The Next American Metropolis

Ecology, Community, and the American Dream

PETER CALTHORPE

Guidelines with Shelley Poticha

Princeton Architectural Press

Published by
Princeton Architectural Press
37 East 7th Street
New York, New York 10003

04 03 02 01 99 98 97   10 9 8 7 6 5

Printed and bound in Canada

Library of Congress Cataloging-in-Publication Data
Calthorpe, Peter.
    The next American metropolis: ecology, community, and the
American dream / Peter Calthorpe.
        p.   cm.
    ISBN 1-878271-68-7 :
    1. City planning—United States. 2. Urban ecology—United States.
3. Metropolitan areas—United States. I. Title.
HT167.C3 1993
307.76'0973—dc20   93-10170
                                                         CIP

Acknowledgements

A decade ago, I wrote a book with Sim Van der Ryn called *Sustainable Communities*. It was the result of years of research and experimentation into the relationship between design and the environment. The underlying precept for me then, and now, is that environmentally benign places and technologies are fundamentally more humane and richer than those which are demanding and destructive of natural ecosystems. We had worked through the seventies to demonstrate that architecture could prove this point – that naturally ventilated, daylit, and solar heated buildings were both efficient and delightful. We also realized that the structure of our physical community could be seen in the same light. That book was the beginning of an effort to define the form and technologies of communities which could be environmentally benign, economically efficient, and socially robust. It was a first attempt to integrate many disciplines in order to define alternatives for urban, suburban, and new growth conditions.

Although that work defined the environmental and technical basis of sustainable communities, it failed to incorporate the "urbanism" which makes communities socially vibrant and alive. By urbanism I do not mean city-like densities and highrise buildings, I mean the qualities of community design which establish diversity, pedestrian scale, and public identity regardless of location or density. It failed to articulate the form of such an urbanism—the detail of building, street, park, and community center which could become the building block of a more environmental city. My work since that time has been an effort to complete that picture and find the forms which could integrate urbanism and environmentalism.

There have been many who have participated in this search at the theoretical level. First, Mark Mack joined me in an NEA grant to develop the concepts of "Pedestrian Pockets." The concepts evolved over the last six years in design studios at UC Berkeley and through many design "charrettes" sponsored by Doug Kelbaugh, chairman of the Architecture Department at the University of Washington. Doug's efforts have been central to the evolution of the ideas in academia and in practice. One of the design charrettes he organized was summarized in the booklet *The Pedestrian Pocket Book* published in 1990. At the University of California at Berkeley, design studios studying these concepts were run by Lars Lerup, Mark Mack, Sim Van der Ryn, and, most aggressively, Dan Solomon. Dan's work both in studio and in practice has been a great inspiration to me. He, along with Andres Duany, Elizabeth Plater-Zyberk, Anne Tate, Dave Sellers, Jonathon Rose, and Stefanos Polyzoides, have formed a community of common cause which, through sharing ideas and problems, has become an invaluable source of support and camaraderie. Andres' and Lizz' work continues to challenge and inform me while their friendship reinforces a sense of shared goals.

The first translation of these ideas from the theoretical to the real is largely due to Phil Angelides' vision and risk taking. As a major developer in the Sacramento area he decided to redesign one of his largest projects, forgoing the easy path of replication, investing in new ideas, and testing the market for a new type of suburban community. Not only did he and his partners take the risk, but his insight about design, the development process, and the nature of community greatly expanded the then-germinating concepts. The experiment he started is still ongoing at Laguna West.

There have been many others who have chosen to strike out in this new direction, but several are worth noting because they represent models of how change can come about. The Environmental Council of Sacramento, rather than taking the typical environmentalist's tactic of merely reacting to development proposals, took the time to seek out and communicate an alternative. They led by publishing a "white paper" on alternatives to sprawl for the Sacramento region which ultimately resulted in the county incorporating the concepts into their General Plan. Similarly, the planning staff of Sacramento County did not take the easy path when they built that General Plan on the TOD concept, but they certainly advanced thinking in the profession. San Diego, under the progressive leadership of Mike Stepner, has also advanced the state of the art by developing an unmatched community participation process to bring about new development guidelines in that growing city. Finally, another environmental group, 1000 Friends of Oregon, has recently helped break new ground by sponsoring a major study which not only demonstrates an alternate to sprawl, but quantified the differences and updated the analysis tools needed to adequately judge those differences. Henry Richmond, their founder and director, has been a pioneer in the environmental community with the board and inclusionary thinking he brings to environmental causes.

Along with these pioneering clients there have been many professionals who have participated in each project, advanced the work, and educated all of us. Ken Kay is both a landscape architect and planner who has worked side by side with me on some of our most important efforts. Growing out of extensive private practice and vision, his design skill and empathy for progressive ideas has complemented and enhanced everything we have collaborated on. His work on Laguna West has made the reality of the project better than the concept. Jack Peers is a traffic engineer who over time has come to understand, document, and advocate a new direction in thinking about travel behavior and the design of circulation systems. His insights and conformation have helped overcome the relentless obstructions of many single-minded engineers. Economics are the bottom line for every development, and Jim Musbach has worked time and time again to show how these new patterns can work fiscally and ultimately as better investments than standard sprawl. Finally I must acknowledge David Beers who, through a rare act of advocacy journalism, first published these ideas and thereby catalyzed much of what has come to pass. These individuals, and many others who have collaborated with us over the years, have all helped demonstrate the value and strength of a multi-disciplinary approach to community design.

Foremost I must thank my staff and associates, Shelley Poticha, Phil Erickson, Matt Taecker, Rick Williams, Cleve Brakefield, Joe Scanga, Catherine Chang, Emily Keenan, and Maya Foty. They have in all ways aided and advanced the work with their creativity, diligence, and insight. Shelley Poticha has not only worked to edit and clarify this book but also has written large segments of the Guidelines. Rick Williams was my associate and co-designer for many of the projects shown here. His design expertise spans architecture to planning in a rare and energetic fashion. Phil Erickson shares his role and design talents with an added capacity to manage large and complex projects. Matt Taecker, a recent associate, is another of a new breed of practitioners who understands planning and can also design. They all have been both a source and the realization of the ideals and principles laid forth here.

In addition there are many who have helped directly with this book. Marianne Wyss provided a remarkable combination of graphic design skill and patience in producing a book of constantly changing content. Shelley Poticha, Matt Taecker, and Phil Erickson have been my in-house editors, both critiquing ideas as they emerge through the work and providing first-pass edits of the manuscript. Catherine Chang has had primary responsibility for pulling together all the graphic material throughout the book, a monumental task handled with grace and skill. And I have been fortunate to have had two extraordinary editors, Chris Dresser and Doug Foster, who have helped a designer through the painful process of partially learning to write. Finally, I must thank Jean Driscoll for her sometimes painful but always insightful readings and thoughts.

To Phil Angelides whose combination of idealism and pragmatism helped translate theory into practice. And to my son, Asa, who always reminds me what neighborhoods are for.

Contents

Introduction

This book is about the American Metropolis; by which I mean the sum total of the city, its suburbs, and their natural environment. The three are inseparable and the failure to treat them as a whole is endemic to many of our problems. Our impact on the natural environment is dependent on the type of settlements we form and the technologies which serve them. The way we build suburbs effects the viability and vitality of our city centers. And the quality of our cities effects the cultural underpinnings of the American Dream and therefore the nature and location of the growth we choose. They are each interdependent and connected at the root by our concept of community.

This book is about the ecology of communities. Not about the ecology of natural systems – but about how the ecological principles of diversity, interdependence, scale, and decentralization can play a role in our concept of suburb, city, and region. It is about communities more diverse and integrated in use and population; more walkable and human-scaled; communities which openly acknowledge and formalize the decentralization at work in our times. These principles stand in stark contrast to a world dominated by specialization, segregation, lack of scale, and centralization. The blend and balance of these opposites is at the core of how we choose to shape the man-made environment. I believe a new blend and balance is overdue.

Finally, this book is about who we are, how our patterns of settlement affect our economy and environment, and, most importantly, how things can change. New models for the metropolis and the design of community are at the heart of this work – models derived from personal values and practical experience, models which seek to restore the best of our oldest traditions of town planning and join them to forms appropriate to our new conditions. With these models for community and region come new possibilities for the city, the suburbs, and the environment. Periodically, America reinvents itself, simultaneously rediscovering the best of its past and marrying it to irresistible forces for change. I believe that time is now.

The suburb was the driving force of the post-WWII era, the physical expression of the privatization of life and specialization of place which marks our time. The result of this era is that both the city and suburb are now locked in a mutually negating evolution toward loss of community, human scale, and nature. In practical terms, these patterns of growth have created on one side congestion, pollution, and isolation, and on the other urban disinvestment and economic hardship.

We can easily quantify the physical problems of suburban sprawl. But this leads too easily to the sense that we can engineer a solution. Both symptoms and causes are complex, involving history, habits, and dreams as well as infrastructure and economics. The question of cultural and social determinism in relation to planning has been debated endlessly – to no conclusive result. Unfortunately, it is just as simplistic to claim that the form of communities has no impact on human behavior as it is to claim that we can prescribe behavior by physical design. For example, a recent comparison study of ten-year-olds in a small town in Vermont and a new suburb of Orange County showed that the Vermont kids had three times the mobility (distance and places they could get to on their own) while the Orange County kids watched four times as much TV. Is this physical determinism or a cultural difference? The two come to be inseparable. Certainly the Orange County kids had fewer mobility alternatives given the physical structure of their neighborhoods, but their culture and peer group priorities may also have directed their behavior. Or perhaps the technology, cable TV, played the decisive role.

So it is easy to talk quantitatively about the physical and environmental consequences of continued sprawl, but very difficult to postulate their social implications. Many argue that there is no longer a causal relationship between the structure of our physical environment and human well-being or social health. We are adaptable and our communities are formed around interest groups and work rather than any sense of place or history. Our lives are more abstract, less grounded in place, and our social forms are now disconnected from home and neighborhood. While some have proposed a rigorous return to traditional city forms and an almost pre-industrial culture as a counterpoint, others have praised this placeless evolution of the suburban megalopolis. They claim it is the inevitable and desirable expression of our new technologies and hyper-individualized culture.

This praise of the status quo is reinforced by the belief that design can't change human behavior. Simply stated, building walkable neighborhoods may not get people out of their cars and building front porches and neighborhood parks may not create more integrated, convivial communities. To this I can only assert that people should be given the choice and that, neither black nor white, the result will probably be mixed – and that is OK. People are not simple and we should not attempt to make them so with cities and suburbs that limit their choices. I believe a diverse and inclusionary environment filled with alternative ways of getting around is inherently better than a world of private enclaves dominated by the car.

Along with this sticky question of physical and social form is the erroneous belief that our community's physical form is the result of free choice, the market's wisdom, and the statistical sum of our collective will. In reality, our patterns of growth are as much a result of public policy and subsidies, outdated regulations, environmental forces, technology, and simple inertia as they are a result of the invisible hand of Adam Smith. These forces are like the postulates from which the formulas of our communities are derived. Change one and a new geometry emerges; change several and a new set of alternatives to the way we live and the places we inhabit becomes possible. As these postulates change with the coming of the next century we must attend to the new geometries that emerge and make sure that they form communities that are equitable, sustainable, and inclusive.

Because the social linkages are complex, the practical must come first: land, energy, and resources should be saved, traffic should be reduced, homes should be more affordable, children and the elderly should have more access, and working people should not be burdened with long commutes. These are quantitative effects that have been demonstrated in many of our older neighborhoods, towns, and cities today – and, I believe, can be updated in new developments to match our current conditions. The social consequences of such changes are less quantitative or deterministic, but perhaps equally compelling. They have to do with the quality of our shared world, aesthetics of place, and the social health of our communities.

My perspective and knowledge in this area is largely gathered from a professional practice which combines architecture, urban design, and land use planning. Therefore it lacks the focus of an academic theory or the rigor of analysis and documentation that a specialist can debate. But the work and concepts are practical – they are used every day by clients, elected officals, technicians, and ultimately the marketplace. To date they have been tested in community planning projects that total over 100,000 acres and range from urban infill to new towns, from comprehensive plans for major cities to individual buildings. The results are only radical in their effort to integrate the elements of community currently isolated in both thought and design process; only radical in their effort to respond to current conditions rather than perpetuate models of the past.

In my work there is no possibility of being a specialist. Every project has a political, economic, ecological, social, technical, aesthetic, and ideological dimension. When designing communities these concerns should be inseparable. But architects, planners, landscape architects, traffic engineers, civil engineers, biologists, developers, environmentalists, bankers, and even neighborhood groups too often seek to optimize only a segment, an issue, or an individual system. This work is an attempt to show that community design must be multi-disciplinary and that combining problems often leads to simple solutions while segregating problems typically leads to frustration.

The model presented in this book may seem at times too specific, technical, or too focused on transit. It is meant to be specific and technical in order to go beyond the pleasing policy statements which fill planning documents but are typically lost in implementation. Its focus on transit is meant to broaden a larger movement – Neo-Traditional Planning and the New Urbanism – which has many dimensions and differing emphasis.

These approaches share fundamental principles but set out in slightly different directions. I have tried to focus my work into a tool that can be used for the larger structuring of a region as well as the detailed design of a neighborhood. As such, it modifies the treatment of the neighborhood with the perspective of a regionalism based on conservation and transit, rather than sprawl and the car. With regards to all these proposals, it is important to remember that there is no absolute template and that the specifics of place, economics, and politics will always color and balance the different directions.

This book is part polemic, part tool, part proof by assertion, part manifesto, but mostly, I hope, common sense. Beneath the rationales, facts, examples, and guidelines is a simple ethos. This ethos provides a specific aesthetic of place – scaled to the human body, timed to a stride, patterned to ceremony, and bonded to nature. It is an aesthetic grounded in the notion that space is not an infinite grid, that time is not relentlessly progressive, that pattern is not formally mechanical, and that boundaries are not limits.

This aesthetic of place has four dimensions: scale, pace, pattern, and bounds. Our built environment clearly delineates these dimensions for our culture. The scale of our environment is now set in proportion to large institutions and bureaucracies rather than community and neighborhood. The pace is set by electronic sound bites and the auto rather than human breath and step. The pattern is established by mass production and discontinuous ownership rather than local craft and social continuity. And the bounds are set by wealth and power rather than proportion and nature. Some argue that this is a "brave new world" created from the technologies and economies that express our deepest desires and ambitions. Even if this were true, the problem is that there is simply not enough of it to go around and that it is consuming its own future – if not all futures.

This is not to argue that a personal aesthetic is the foundation of this work. Many forces converge; social impacts, economic sustainability, political implications, and environmental limits all focus toward a fundamental change. Aesthetics in its largest sense is a summation and distillation of these forces. Social integration, economic efficiency, political equity, and environmental sustainability are the imperatives which order my thinking about the form of community. Each of these imperatives has causes and implications beyond the physical form of community, but community form remains a central expression of and reinforcement to the underlying culture.

The foundation of our current aesthetic of place is Modernism. Across political ideology, modernism defines the fundamental nature of our times: segregation, specialization, centralization, and an undying dedication to technology. Implicit is its sense of progress and the ideology of materialism. It is systemic to almost all western cultures, beyond national borders, political structure, or cultural values. Modernism is clearly expressed by the evolution of cities and regions in the twentieth century: the segregation of activities and peoples, the specialization and isolation of professions and the systems they create, the centralization of ever-larger institutions, and the monopoly of certain technologies, most notably the car.

In many fields there has been a movement away from Modernist principles. In architecture and design Post Modern theory began to evolve in the early 1970s. It attempted to relearn from history the traditions in architecture and urban design which preserved human scale and urban identity in community. Unfortunately, it hasn't live up to its potential. Rather than defining a new direction and an alternate set of principles, it merely cast a new veneer over our old Modernist structure. It reinforces the modernist tendency toward specialization: facades by architects, environmental systems by mechanical engineers, site design by civil engineers, open space by landscape architects, and the urban environment by traffic engineers and politicians. The desire to re-establish history, place, and community has been reduced to nostalgic facades and sarcastic historicism at the surface of buildings. Post Modernism has been deflected from a real restructuring of the man-made environment to the architectural equivalent of a marketing gimmick. The Modernist landscape of buildings isolated from the environment and any urban vitality remains unchanged, except in costume.

Against this false dichotomy of Modernism and Post Modernism ecology has come to represent, for me, the real counterpoint. Not the literal ecology which deals with natural systems and seems to stop just short of the human habitat – but a broader, more philosophic "ecology" which teaches that diversity, interdependence, and whole systems are fundamental to health. It is this perspective and the attempt to translate it into specific form for our buildings and communities which has directed my work. It has been an interesting search, not altogether free of mistakes and always full of the next question.

This book moves from the general to the specific. In the first section the philosophical and practical reasoning behind the work is articulated. It is the description of the way things are, and *why* they must change. The second section, in the form of guidelines, describes *how* they can change. It is both a detailed description of an urban strategy and a design tool which can be used in many circumstances. In this sense I owe a debt to Chris Alexander, who in his *Pattern Language* created a model of design guidelines which both educated and informed while providing a specific tool to be used in the design process.

Finally the section on projects demonstrates the application of the principles and guidelines to a range of projects from regional planning to small infill sites. These projects have been presented primarily in plan rather than with renderings or perspectives. This was done to simplify the reading and cross-referencing of the differing scales, and partly to sidestep the complex business of architectural language. It is the thesis of this work that Urban Design – the public quality of buildings and their interrelationships – must be clarified before an architecture can function. It is my belief that the architecture of these places is not as important as the urban order and the quality of their public spaces. Put simply, buildings can be ordinary if they are part of a beautiful street or square and in fact it may be important for more buildings to be "ordinary." In the American town, architecture is eclectic and of an uneven quality – and I hope it will remain so. This eclecticism can be chaotic if built without a sound urban framework or it can be delightful when placed within a strong system of legible and memorable public places.

From where I sit in San Francisco, a major urban transformation seems imminent. Less than twenty percent of the people living in the Bay Area today can afford a median-priced home. People are moving to the Central Valley and commuting three to four hours a day to find affordable housing. Traffic congestion is always on the rise. Citizens are constantly organizing against more of what they believe are the ill effects of growth but are really just the byproducts of sprawl. We must find regional and neighborhood forms which can honor the needs of our diverse population, while safeguarding the environment.

At its base this book is about the infrastructure of community, rather than isolation. Hopefully it provides the counterpoint to the landscape of specialization and separation that our suburbs have become – a counterpoint which could make the debate and final decision between these directions meaningful. As the ideas presented here have been implemented, they have become less pure, more contextual, and, some claim, compromised. Design becomes "the art of the possible." This, in the end, is what interests me most; the intersection between an ideal and the real world. I believe we need both, utopians and engineers, visions and constraints, liberty and responsibility – a new American Dream and a new American Metropolis.

THE NEXT AMERICAN METROPOLIS

The American Dream is an evolving image and the American Metropolis is its ever-changing reflection. The two feed one another in a complex, interactive cycle. At one point a dream moves us to a new vision of the city and community, at another the reflection of the city transforms that dream with harsh realities or alluring opportunities. We are at a point of transformation once again and the two, city and dream, are changing together. World War II created a distinct model for each: the nuclear family in the suburban landscape. That model and its physical expression is now stressed beyond retention. The family has grown more complex and diverse, while the suburban form has grown more demanding and less accessible. The need for change is blatant, with sprawl reaching its limits, communities fracturing into enclaves, and families seeking more inclusive identities. Clearly we need a new paradigm of development; a new vision of the American Metropolis and a new image for the American Dream.

The old suburban dream is increasingly out of sync with today's culture. Our household makeup has changed dramatically, the work place and work force have been transformed, average family wealth is shrinking, and serious environmental concerns have surfaced. But we continue to build post-World War II suburbs as if families were large and had only one breadwinner, as if the jobs were all downtown, as if land and energy were endless, and as if another lane on the freeway would end traffic congestion.

Over the last twenty years these patterns of growth have become more and more dysfunctional. Finally they have come to produce environments which often frustrate rather than enhance everyday life. Suburban sprawl increases pollution, saps inner-city development, and generates enormous costs – costs which ultimately must be paid by taxpayers, consumers, businesses, and the environment. The problems are not to be solved by limiting the scope, program, or location of development – they must be resolved by rethinking the nature and quality of growth itself, in every context.

This book attempts to map out a new direction for growth in the American Metropolis. It borrows from many traditions and theories: from the romantic environmentalism of Ruskin to the City Beautiful Movement, from the medieval urbanism of Sitte to the Garden Cities of Europe, from streetcar suburbs to the traditional towns of America, and from the theories of Jane Jacobs to those of Leon Krier. It is a work which has evolved from theory to practice in some of our fastest growing cities and regions. It is a search for a paradigm that combines the utopian ideal of an integrated and heterogeneous community with the realities of our time – the imperatives of ecology, affordability, equity, technology, and the relentless force of inertia. The work asserts that our communities must be designed to reestablish and reinforce the public domain, that our districts must be human-scaled, and that our neighborhoods must be diverse in use and population. And finally, that the form and identity of the metropolis must integrate historic context, unique ecologies, and a comprehensive regional structure.

The net result is that we need to start creating neighborhoods rather than subdivisions; urban quarters rather than isolated projects; and diverse communities rather than segregated master plans. Quite simply, we need towns rather than sprawl.

Settlement patterns are the physical foundation of our society and, like our society, they are becoming more and more fractured. Our developments and local zoning laws segregate age groups, income groups, and ethnic groups, as well as family types. Increasingly they isolate people and activities in an inefficient network of congestion and pollution – rather than joining them in diverse and human scaled communities. Our faith in government and the fundamental sense of commonality at the center of any vital democracy is seeping away in suburbs designed more for cars than people, more for market segments than communities. Special interest groups have now replaced citizens in the political landscape, just as gated subdivisions have replaced neighborhoods.

Redefining the American Dream

It is time to redefine the American Dream. We must make it more accessible to our diverse population: singles, the working poor, the elderly, and the pressed middle-class families who can no longer afford the "Ozzie and Harriet" version of the good life. Certain traditional values – diversity, community, frugality, and human scale – should be the foundation of a new direction for both the American Dream and the American Metropolis. These values are not a retreat to nostalgia or imitation, but a recognition that certain qualities of culture and community are timeless. And that these timeless imperatives must be married to the modern condition in new ways.

The alternative to sprawl is simple and timely: neighborhoods of housing, parks, and schools placed within walking distance of shops, civic services, jobs, and transit – a modern version of the traditional town. The convenience of the car and the opportunity to walk or use transit can be blended in an environment with local access for all the daily needs of a diverse community. It is a strategy which could preserve open space, support transit, reduce auto traffic, and create affordable neighborhoods. Applied at a regional scale, a network of such mixed-use neighborhoods could create order in our balkanized metropolis. It could balance inner-city development with suburban investment by organizing growth around an expanding transit system and setting defensible urban limit lines and greenbelts. The increments of growth in each neighborhood would be small, but the aggregate could accommodate regional growth with minimal environmental impacts; less land consumed, less traffic generated, less pollution produced.

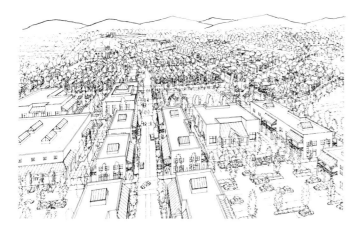

Such neighborhoods, called Pedestrian Pockets or Transit-Oriented Developments, ultimately could be more affordable for working families, environmentally responsible, and cost-effective for business and government. But, such a growth strategy will mean fundamentally changing our preconceptions and local regulatory priorities, as well as redesigning the federal programs that shape our cities.

At the core of this alternative, philosophically and practically, is the pedestrian. Pedestrians are the catalyst which makes the essential qualities of communities meaningful. They create the place and the time for casual encounters and the practical integration of diverse places and people. Without the pedestrian, a community's common ground – its parks, sidewalks, squares, and plazas – become useless obstructions to the car. Pedestrians are the lost measure of a community, they set the scale for both center and edge of our neighborhoods. Without the pedestrian, an area's focus can be easily lost. Commerce and civic uses are easily decentralized into distant chain store destinations and government centers. Homes and jobs are isolated in subdivisions and office parks.

Although pedestrians will not displace the car anytime soon, their absence in our thinking and planning is a fundamental source of failure in our new developments. To plan as if there were pedestrians may be a self-fulfilling act; it will give kids some autonomy, the elderly basic access, and others the choice to walk again. To plan as if there were pedestrians will turn suburbs into towns, projects into neighborhoods, and networks into communities.

If we are now to reinvest in America, careful consideration should be given to what kind of America we want to create. Our investments in transit must be supported by land use patterns which put riders and jobs within an easy walk of stations. Our investments in affordable housing should place families in neighborhoods where they can save dollars by using their autos less. Our investments in open space should reinforce regional greenbelts and urban limit lines. Our investments in highways should not unwittingly support sprawl, inner-city disinvestment, or random job decentralization. Our investments in inner-cities and urban businesses ought to be linked by transit to the larger region, not isolated by gridlock. Our planning and zoning codes should help create communities, not sprawl.

Is such a transformation possible? Americans love their cars, they love privacy and independence, and they are evolving ever larger institutions. The goal of community planning for the pedestrian or transit is not to eliminate the car, but to balance it. In the 1970s the national love affair with the car was certainly hot, but we traveled on average 50 percent fewer miles per year than we do now. It *is* possible to accommodate the car and still free pedestrians. Practically, it means narrowing local roads and placing parking to the rear of buildings, not eliminating access for the car. Similarly, the suburban goals of privacy and independence do not have to be abandoned in the interests of developing communities with vital urban centers and neighborly streets. In fact, a walkable neighborhood may produce increased independence for growing segments of the population, the elderly and kids. The scale of our institutions may no longer fit the human scale proportions of an old village, but with careful design they could be integrated into mixed-use communities. Large businesses are quickly becoming aware of the benefits of being part of a neighborhood rather than an office park, with shared amenities and local services topping the list.

This new balance calls for the integration of seemingly opposing forces. Community and privacy, auto and pedestrian, large institution and small business, suburban and urban; these are the poles that must be fused in a new pattern of growth. The design imperatives of creating the post-suburban metropolis are complex and challenging. They are to develop a regional growth strategy which integrates social diversity, environmental protection, and transit; create an architecture that reinforces the public domain without sacrificing the variety and character of individual buildings; advance a planning approach that reestablishes the pedestrian in mixed-use, livable communities; and evolve a design philosophy that is capable of accommodating modern institutions without sacrificing human scale and memorable places.

The Crisis of Place in America

There is a growing sense of frustration and placelessness in our suburban landscape; a homogeneous quality which overlays the unique nature of each place with chain-store architecture, scaleless office parks, and monotonous subdivisions. These qualities are easily blurred by the speed we move and the isolation we feel in our cars and in our dwellings. At its extreme, the new forms seem to have a restless and hollow feel, reinforcing our mobile state and perhaps the instability of our families. Moving at a speed which only allows generic symbols to be recognized, we cannot wonder that the manmade environment seems trite and overstated. Americans moved to the suburbs largely for privacy, mobility, security, and ownership. Increasingly they now have isolation, congestion, rising crime, and overwhelming costs. Meanwhile our city centers have deteriorated as much of their economic vitality has decanted to the suburbs.

A LANDSCAPE OF ISOLATION

At the same time that suburban growth falls short of its promise, its premise is shifting. There is now a striking mismatch between the suburban patterns of settlement that have evolved since World War II and our current "postindustrial" culture. It is at the root of many regional ills: serious environmental stress, intractable traffic congestion, a dearth of affordable housing, loss of irreplaceable open space, and lifestyles which burden working families and isolate the elderly. This mismatch has two primary sources: a fundamental change in the character of our households and a dramatic shift in the nature and location of our workplace.

Our suburbs are designed around a stereotypical household which is no longer predominant. The size of households has been shrinking, from an average of three twenty years ago to two and a half today. The percentage of singles and single-parent families is increasing, from 29 percent twenty years ago to 38 percent today. Of the approximately 17 million new households formed in the 1980s, 51 percent were occupied by single people and unrelated individuals, 22 percent by single-parent families, and only 27 percent by married couples with or without children. People over 65 made up 23 percent of those total new households. Households with children typically now have two workers. Married couples with children now represent only 26 percent of the households, down from 40 percent a generation ago.

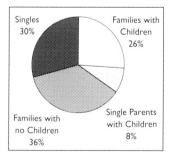

HOUSEHOLD COMPOSITION: 1990

And the economics of the household has changed. Working mothers are becoming the norm with double-income households now representing 54 percent of all families. Women are certainly less available to support a suburban family lifestyle which requires a chauffeur for every child's trip. Add to this the escalating cost of housing and the needs of working women, and the possibility of realizing the old American Dream in existing development patterns becomes increasingly unlikely.

Even these double-income families now find home ownership a troublesome, if not unattainable, goal. With affordable housing growing ever more elusive, families have to move to cheaper but more distant peripheral areas, often consuming irreplaceable agricultural land and overloading roads with long commutes. In 1970 about half of all families could afford a median-priced single-family home; today less than a quarter can.

Beneath the statistics is a more profound change in the structure of family and the role of women in our society. Many have argued that the role of women in the suburbs of the fifties and sixties was oppressive. The model of isolated homemaker, on-call chauffeur, and sole daycare provider may have helped germinate the feminist movement that followed. Whether liberation, necessity, or ambition, the entry of women into the workforce changed the cultural landscape dramatically. And of course it transformed the needs of home, neighborhood, and community. Many now understand that without a full-time caretaker the suburban dream cannot function. "Latch-key kids" and "bedroom communities" describe conditions that no longer fit the needs of our families. We need communities that are occupied full time and that provide a world of opportunity for kids, communities that support women (and men) in their efforts to weave together an ever more complex life of home and work.

The nature and location of the workplace has also changed. As the computer has allowed new jobs to shift from blue-collar to white and gray, employment centers have de-centralized into mammoth lowrise office parks on cheap and often remote sites. The shift is dramatic and has far-reaching consequences. From 1973 to 1985 five million blue-collar jobs were lost nationwide, while service fields gained from 82 to 110 million jobs. This translated directly into 1.1 billion square feet of office space constructed in new suburban employment complexes. Nationwide, these complexes have moved outside the

central cities with the percentage of total office space in the suburbs shifting from 25 percent in 1970 to 57 percent in 1984.

Traffic congestion in the suburbs is a signal of this deep shift in the structure of our economic culture. The growth of the service industry has led to this decentralization of the workplace, causing new traffic patterns and "suburban gridlock." Where downtown employment once dominated, suburb-to-suburb traffic patterns now produce greater commute distances and driving time. Over 40 percent of all commute trips are now from suburb to suburb. These new patterns have seriously eroded the quality of life in formerly quiet suburban towns. In the San Francisco Bay Area, for example, as in many metropolitan areas around the country, 212 miles of the region's 812 miles of suburban freeway are regularly backed up during rush hours. That figure is projected to double within the next 12 years. As a result, recent polls have traffic continually heading the list as the primary regional problem, followed closely by the difficulty of finding good affordable housing.

Congestion and high housing costs are not the only economic measure of the cost of sprawl. American employers – public and private – face compensation demands that reflect high transportation and housing costs. Worker productivity slides with congestion and long commutes. Raw material and product movement is costly and uncertain. Air quality standards often restrict industrial growth as pollution from cars "uses up" the air shed. Add to these factors the time cost of getting a building permit for expansion or new facilities, and a region's ability to maintain a healthy job base erodes. This is a circumstance not caused just by local citizen opposition to growth, but by the failure of American public policy to set a clear, reliable, and sustainable land use direction.

The problems of suburbia feed back to our city centers. Increas-

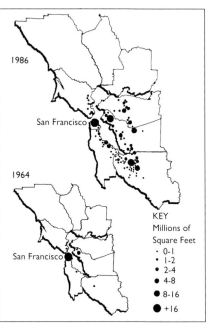

KEY
Millions of
Square Feet
· 0-1
· 1-2
· 2-4
● 4-8
● 8-16
● +16

DISTRIBUTION OF BAY AREA OFFICE SPACE

ing decay and economic isolation have resulted from forty years of job flight and racial isolation. These problems and their motivations are, of course, complex and well beyond the control of land planning prescriptions. But the impact of federal policies that invest more in suburbs than in cities cannot be overlooked. Beyond the obvious subsidies of highway spending and mortgage tax incentives, the suburbs have benefited from the location of a majority of defense contract jobs over the last twenty years and indirectly benefited from the S&L bailout (to the extent that tax dollars are now paying for the past ten years of booming suburban construction). As long as cheap, clean suburban land is made accessible through unrestrained zoning practices and federal highway dollars, the inner city will continue to suffer from disinvestment.

There is a vicious cycle at work in our inner cities. The more development and tax base decants to the suburbs, the less attractive the inner city becomes to investors, business or homeowners. In the Washington DC metropolitian region for example, it has been estimated that 210 million square feet of new commercial and residential development are needed to pay off the existing municipal bonds, including the $10 billion METRO transit system. Although there is space for three quarters of this development around existing suburban transit stations and within the city, little of it is locating there. The tax revenues that would have come with development are leaking away. Because development and tax base is escaping, pressing urban problems, such as housing, crime, and AIDS are underfunded, leading to an urban environment unattractive to investment of any type. The inner city will not get the development investment or tax dollars its urban citizens need partly because the region is allowed to sprawl. Two complementary strategies are needed. A tough regional plan which limits sprawl and channels development back to the city or around suburban transit stations; and a matching greenbelt strategy to preserve open space at the edge of the region. We cannot revitalize inner cities without changing the patterns of growth at the periphery of metropolitan regions; it is a simple matter of the finite distribution of resources.

The working poor of our cities are at a double disadvantage. They cannot afford to move to the suburbs, and in many cases, they cannot even afford to commute there. The high cost of housing in large-lot, apartment-short suburbia is an economic wall for the working poor, as it is increasingly for the children of suburbanites. In addition, the inadequacy of public bus or rail transportation to suburbia reduces access for the working poor to the decentralized but growing suburban job centers. With an increasing proportion of urban disposable income going to pay for housing, few can afford an extra car to get to a suburban job. In Central Los Angeles an average 71 percent of household income goes to pay for housing. In the central areas of Portland, Oregon, due to a mix of economic constraints and personal preference, 40 percent of households do not own a car.

In contrast, the typical suburban home now has 2.3 cars and generates 12 auto trips per day. The increasingly lower density development patterns that generate those trips have pushed up vehicle miles traveled (VMT) three times faster than population growth for four decades. Our nation's sprawl-generated transportation "system" burns up 69 percent of the nation's oil, half of which is now imported.

Our urban-suburban split has created on one side disinvestment and economic hardship, on the other congestion and pollution. The crisis of place in America affects everyone in that it fails to fulfill the real needs of so many. But in defining an alternate we must clearly distinguish the physical problems and solutions from the social and cultural.

The Traditional American Town

What are the alternatives? Just as we cannot sustain the crisis of place represented by sprawl, we cannot return wholesale to the form and scale of the pre-WWII American town. We cannot simply return to a time in were people walked, the shopkeepers lived upstairs, and neighbors were all on first-name basis. For one thing, the auto, modern suburbia's form giver, will not retreat even if constrained and balanced by land use alternatives. The extended family and mom and-pop-shops will not return regardless of design controls or clever planning. And unfortunately, the varied craftsman-like architecture built in small increments is largely a thing of the past. But more finely integrated, walkable communities with a strong local identity and convivial public places are possible. The forms of these places will and should vary in time and place, but certain design principles will emerge as both timeless and contemporary. Timeless in the sense that human needs and human scale do not change with the advent of each new technology and that certain traditions express fundamental characteristics of place and culture which should be preserved. The traditional American town still demonstrates many of these principles; principles which can be adapted to the contemporary situation.

AFFORDABLE BUNGALOWS AT LAGUNA WEST

The traditional American town had walkable streets. Streets that led to close and useful destinations rather than – like our modern collectors and high traffic arterials – only to other streets. Elm Street led to Main Street, or to the neighborhood park, or daycare or an elementary school. Such a street pattern is actually cheaper to build and results in shorter trip distances even if people don't walk. The streets were narrow, with sidewalks, and tree-lined. They were fronted by porches, balconies, and entries rather than garage doors and driveways. They allowed through traffic but slowed it with frequent intersections and frugal dimensions. There were no collector streets, complete with soundwalls, and cul-de-sacs. Privacy was maintained through layers of space rather than barriers. Security was provided by eyes on the street rather than gates and patrols. Today, such streets would be practical, not merely nostalgic; practical for single parents in need of some mobility for their kids; for the elderly without a car; for the single person looking for accessibility; and for the working family looking for a stronger community.

The traditional American town had diversity of use and users. So does the modern suburb, but in a different, highly segregated form. It is true that the classic town distinctly separated many uses: residential neighborhoods, commercial areas, school sites, and civic centers. But the connections between uses were internal and walkable, close and direct. And the population was diverse in age, income, and family size. These groups may have been physically separated in the traditional American town, but the connections were accessible and they all shared an identifiable commercial center and civic focus.

The center of the traditional town integrated commercial, recreational, and civic life. It was what made a town a town. Main Street was a strollable connector between these pieces. The same integration is possible today, although not common. We have zoned each use into isolated and unrelated sites; a civic "center" complex often away from the historic town center, shopping "centers" at arterial crossroads, and parks on cheap and remote parcels. Bringing these pieces back together can do more than create identity and focus for a community, it can acually enhance the function of each use.

Imagine a village green with daycare, recreation, and a town hall surrounded by homes and fronted on one side by a retail center. The retail center would be directly accessible from the neighborhood and an arterial roadway. This area would contain libraries, post office, and professional offices as well as a transit station. The commercial center would clearly benefit from increased patronage created by civic and recreation users, along with transit activity and local residents. The civic buildings would be more accessible if located at such a hub of activity and within walking distance of residential areas. And the park and recreational facilities could be used by shoppers, on-site workers, transit riders, and of course neighborhood kids. The form of such a mixed-use center may not literally mimic the Main Street of our traditional town, but new configurations are possible which incorporate the functional needs of our modern institutions and businesses while respecting pedestrian space.

Some of the characteristics of the traditional town – its fine grain and scale – cannot be adapted. We now have larger institutions which resist decentralization. Retail markets are growing larger, with the typical supermarket pushing 60,000 sq-ft and discount stores reaching 120,000 sq-ft. Small shops remain but the underlying trend is toward the convenience of "one stop shopping" or the scale of price discount. These "anchors," the ever-larger distribution facilities, will resist a Main Street configuration, demanding the market area and visibility of a major arterial. So hybrid town centers should combine the intimacy of Main Street with the accessibility of strip centers. From the neighborhood side, the commercial center must be pedestrian-friendly, from the arterial it must be auto convenient.

The scale – of development entities, builders, and land assembly – has also expanded dramatically in the last 30 years. Towns no longer grow by individual buildings or even small groups, but by production units of approximately 150 houses or by retail centers often of 160,000 sq-ft. Apartments are rarely developed at under one hundred units because of management economics. Land developers now typically seek permits for over 100 acres (the size of a classic town center) with one master plan. Rather than the architectural diversity of incremental growth, we have large blocks of development with formula configurations dictated by the past successes of each developer and by conservative financing criteria. These sizable developments deserve innovative design if they are to avoid the "theme" quality of isolated subdivisions, shopping centers, and office parks. The new Amercian city requires a new architecture capable of integrating these contemporary pieces into a larger community without nostalgically imitating the scale and diversity of older towns. Simultaneously the architecture should avoid the sterility and highway scale of the modern suburbs. The scale of modern development cannot be ignored, concealed, or denied. But it can be responsive to and contribute to a larger civic order.

There is a fine but important difference between tradition and nostalgia. Traditions are rooted in time-less impulses while being constantly modified by circumstance. Tradition evolves with time and place while holding strong to certain formal, cultural, and personal principles. Nostalgia seeks the security of past forms without the inherent principles. The current interest in the traditional American town can tilt to profound and meaningful principles or merely color suburbia with an old-time style. The difference is in the quality and skill of adaptation.

Our Fractured Commons and the Loss of Public Space

Today the public world is shrunken and fractured. Parks, schools, libraries, post offices, town halls, and civic centers are dispersed, underutilized, and underfunded. Yet these civic elements determine the quality of our shared world and express the value we assign to community. The traditional Commons, which once centered our communities with convivial gathering and meeting places, is increasingly displaced by an exaggerated private domain: shopping malls, private clubs, and gated communities. Our basic public space, the street, is given over to the car and its accommodation, while our private world becomes more and more isolated behind garage doors and walled compounds. Our public space lacks identity and is largely anonymous, while our private space strains toward a narcissistic autonomy. Our communities are zoned black and white, private or public, my space or nobody's.

We must return meaning and stature to the physical expression of our public life. From streets and parks to plazas, village squares, and commercial centers, the Commons defines the meeting ground of a neighborhood and its local identity. Rather than isolated and residual spaces, the Commons should be brought back to the center of our communities and re-integrated into our daily commercial life. Public spaces should provide the fundamental order of our communities and set the limits to our private domain. Our public buildings should be proudly located to add quality, identity, and focus to the fabric of our everyday world.

TOWN HALL, LAGUNA WEST

An important dimension of the Commons was traditionally the marketplace. Ironic that the greatest consumer society in history would evolve a myopic and almost grotesque retail form. Retail centers are now a precise order of types, marketed with misnomers: convenience center, neighborhood center, community center, regional mall, and power center. Each targets a specialized market segment and comes complete with a generic template. The guiding principles of retail are value and convenience. Value leads to ever larger and more remote distribution centers. Convenience has come to simply mean larger parking lots. Human scale and neighborhood focus have been exchanged for auto access and national distribution. Shopping, even at its most incidental scale, is removed from neighborhood and town, removed from the social dimension it used to play in defining a community. Two traditional aspects of commerce have been lost; shopping as an integral part of a community's center and the unique quality of local products and services.

Is the traditional marketplace merely nostalgic and inefficient, or an option currently untested on a population secretly seeking local quality over chain store homogenization? Marketing and advertising has come to displace quality in products much as signage now substitutes for memorable places. Sadly, the way retail developments are financed is a large part of the problem; only chain store operators seem secure investments – local products and shop owners are hard to "package" in large loans. But in the context of mixed-use communities rather than highway strips, human-scaled and local commerce may find fertile ground. There may be a new balance between the realities of the current marketplace and the needs of pedestrians and communities for an indigenous center, rather than a universal formula.

Parks and open space are another essential ingredient of the Commons. At every scale, parks should establish the social increment of place: whether neighborhood, town, or region. Neighborhood parks have become larger and more remote in part to reduce maintenance costs. But for

this small economy the intimate identity of individual neighborhoods is lost. The small park for toddlers, younger children and their parents was once an essential meeting ground as well as a convenience which liberated some kids from being chauffeured to more distant play areas.

On the scale of the town, the village green is rarely considered or used in our modern suburb. This essential piece of the Commons once gave identity to the larger community and acted as the physical glue between residential neighborhoods, commercial center, and civic services. Finally, a network of regional parks and riparian greenways should be a basic element of each metropolitan area. These large scale open spaces, along with the street and transit system, can form the region's connecting network and play a large role in defining the image of place. At each scale identity and connection can be established through what is shared.

The architecture of individual buildings should signal their place in relation to the Commons. Major civic institutions should stand forward as monuments to the community and be assigned special locations. Private and secondary buildings can learn once again the art of humility; they should stand back and reinforce the commons. They must be seen as the "walls" of our outdoor public rooms rather than as isolated, self-referential pieces of sculpture. In a way architects should relearn the art of designing "ordinary" buildings, backdrops to the foreground of public space and civic institution. This relationship of ordinary buildings to public space needs to be reestablished if a basic legibility for the commons is to be achieved.

VILLAGE GREEN

24

Ecology and Community

Communities historically were embedded in nature – it helped set both the unique identity of each place and the physical limits of the community. Local climate, plants, vistas, harbors, and ridgelands once defined the special qualities of every memorable place. Now, smog, pavement, toxic soil, receding ecologies, and polluted water contribute to the destruction of neighborhood and home in the largest sense. We threaten nature and nature threatens us in return: sunlight causes cancer, air threatens our lungs, rain burns the trees, streams are polluted and poisonous, and soil is too often toxic. Understanding the qualities of nature in each place, expressing it in the design of communities, integrating it within our towns, and respecting its balance are essential ingredients of making the human place sustainable and spiritually nourishing.

The design and technology of our communities determines the basic impact we will have on the natural environment. Each system has its impact. Storm drains and parking lots divert water from the land and concentrate the outflow of pollution. Cars turn each outing into more air pollution, congestion, and pavement. Flood control projects sanitize and destroy the complex ecosystems of our riparian zones. Artifical landscapes displace indigenous species with water-demanding imported plant life. Our architecture ignores the benefits of climate-responsive design and consumes more energy than needed. And we allow the constant erosion of agricultural lands and open space at the metropolitan edge. Each of these elements of modern American life, whether by design or the unanticipated effect of our technology, adds to the environmental crisis of growth.

The treatment of water in our communities is a good example of environmental opportunities lost. Rather than using natural water flows and local plants that match the climate, we divert drainage into treatment facilities and select plant species which require imported water. Communities which use their streams and indigenous plants are far more environmentally benign than those which line their waterways with concrete, sealing out the natural world in an all too literal way. They lose the unique quality of place and gain an artificial landscape that could be anywhere. And in the process they pollute and wastewater.

Nature should provide the order and underlying structure of the metropolis. Ridgelands, bays, rivers, ocean, agriculture, and mountains form the inherent boundaries of our regions. They set the natural edge and can become the internal connectors, the larger common ground of place. They should provide the identity and character that unifies the multiplicity of neighborhoods, communities, towns, and cities which now make up our metropolitan regions. Preservation and care for a region's natural ecologies is the fundamental prerequisite of a sustainable and humane urbanism.

Many overlapping types of open space and natural systems shape the metropolis: parks, waterways and flood plains, ridge lands and bays, prime agriculture lands and special habitats. Each operates at a different scale, some defining the larger context of the region, some focusing the identity of a small neighborhood. The effort to create more compact, walkable communities must be complemented with three orders of open space: those that define the edge and limits of the region, those that form a large-scale connecting network within the region, and those that provide identity and recreation within a neighborhood. Each should respect the pre-existing ecology and climate, and each can be a primary form-giver to the region, community, or neighborhood.

At the regional scale, the man-made environment should fit into and along larger natural systems. Urban limit lines or growth boundaries should be set to preserve major natural resources at the edge of the metropolis. This line should be large enough to accommodate growth for the next generation but small enough to encourage infill, redevelopment, and density at the core. Within this regional boundary major natural features and streams should form an internal structure of park-like linkages, trails, and bikeways throughout the metropolis. Such open space elements should link and limit individual communities. In these areas the natural systems should be preserved and repaired.

At the scale of the neighborhood, parks and open space should stop occupying residual space or "buffer" zones between segregated uses. They should be used as formative elements, providing the focus and order of the neighborhood. Neighborhood parks could be smaller and more accessible, and have a strong civic character. Every child should be able to walk safely to a neighborhood park, a park that need not be "naturalist" but should be of the place, socially and ecologically. Such parks can become the foundation of a memo-rable and unique public domain for each neighborhood, community, or town.

There should be nature within our buildings as well as within our communities. This not as simplistic as adding plants and fountains, but a complex imperative to make buildings more climate-responsive. The unique qualities of climate can help define an architecture which is appropriate and frugal in the largest sense. Natural lighting in commercial buildings is a good example. We can save energy and provide more beautiful spaces simply by understanding and using natural light. Rather than reflective glass walls and fluorescent ceilings, clear windows with shades and high ceilings make rooms that can use, instead of reject, natural light. At the same time such buildings make a street edge free of reflected glare and scaleless features. Similarly, natural ventilation and solar heating can animate buildings in ways lost by the sealed boxes of modern architecture. Even simple conservation measures and insulation practices add to a sense of investment and durability in buildings.

Finally, nature is an essential experience of childhood. When we make neighborhoods and towns without nature we destroy the places of fantasy and autonomy that kids need. Leftover land, small and large parks, preserved river banks, open shorelines, and meadow ridges – these are places that become the refuge of the young. The man-made environment is dominated by adults but the natural world, however small, should be a fundamental right of childhood. Kids need enough wilderness to make their own places, and live their own fantasies.

CLIMATE-RESPONSIVE COURTYARD,
BATESON STATE OFFICE BUILDING
SACRAMENTO, CALIFORNIA

The Technology of Mobility

Rather than being guided, as it should be, by natural systems or human needs, the quality and placement of growth in our regions is largely dependent on the car. The car is now the defining technology of our built environment. It sets the form of our cities and town, dictating the scale of streets, the relationship between buildings, the need for vast parking areas, and the speed at which we experience our environment. Somewhere along the continuum from convenience to congestion, the auto dominates what were once diverse streets shared by pedestrians, bikers, shoppers, trolleys, and cars. And more importantly, the auto allows the ultimate segregation of our culture: land uses which separate old from young, home from job and store, rich from poor, and owner from renter. The auto has come to dominate the public realm, extending the private world from garage door to parking lot.

What does the car "want," or for that matter what does a pedestrian or transit system need? The car in all cases wants to go fast. Its speed has many implications on the built environment: pressing for a street system with few intersections and many lanes; for streets with wide lanes and soft sweeping turns; for more freeways and ever-larger parking areas. These criteria result in the curvaceous superblock arterial system, freeway networks, and parking lot landscape so common today. The car wants lots of pavement and the low-density development that preserves plenty of space for more and more asphalt. The car also apparently wants to travel more; between 1969 and 1990 the national population grew by 21 percent while the total vehicle miles traveled in cars increased 82 percent.

But the requirements of a humane and efficient transit system are quite different. It simply requires riders. This in turn calls for higher-density land uses (housing at 10 units per acre min.), dedicated rights-of-way (for easy movement), infrequent station stops (one-mile minimums), frequent headways (no more than 15-minute intervals) and big mixed-use job destinations (like city cores). Most importantly, its destinations need to be varied and walkable so that riders are not stranded when they arrive. Some transit systems have modest requirements, wanting only to serve the poor and carless on an infrequent basis with slow speeds – the "safety net" for those unable to use or afford a car. Other systems are very ambitious, looking for urban densities, high speeds, and uninterrupted underground passageways.

The needs of the pedestrian overlap and in some cases contradict these other systemic constraints. Pedestrians want close destinations: shops, schools, services, or recreation. They need direct links to these destinations free of cul-de-sacs, parking lots, or massive intersections. They want safe, interesting, and comfortable streets to walk on and human scale in the buildings which line it. Simply put, they want narrow streets lined with entries and porches leading to local shops, schools, and parks – not curving streets lined by garage doors leading to six-lane arterials. Pedestrians also like transit to extend their range of destinations. These needs can be satisfied in both high-density urban centers and small mixed use towns, but not in sprawling, unplanned suburbs. The issue is not one of the density of a community but the quality.

Each of these modes of travel places differing demands on the environment and architecture. Clearly, the car places the greatest stress on the environment while "liberating" architecture from the limits of urban context and human scale. At the speed of the auto, little more than isolated signature buildings can be read. Transit calls for an architecture more dense, integrated, and urban than our current planning models require. And the pedestrian wants an architecture oriented to the sidewalk, that creates continuity along with diversity, and that has human scale and detail.

Various environments satisfy different combinations of these contradictory requirements. The European city, for example, works for both the pedestrian and transit, but has great difficulty accommodating the car (hence the many efforts throughout Europe to ban the car in old city cores). The traditional American town provided for both pedestrians and cars (back when there was only one car per house), but rarely offered the density or focus needed for transit. The modern American city, violated by urban renewal, suburban flight, parking structures, and freeway interventions, seems to fully satisfy neither car, transit, nor pedestrian. The modern sub-

urb pleases only the car, leaving both transit systems and the pedestrian frustrated and unsatisfied.

Given the social, economic, and environmental forces of our time, some new synthesis of these three structural demands is needed. The challenge is to introduce the needs of the pedestrian and transit into the auto-dominated regions of our metropolitan areas, and to do so without a fanciful attempt to create faux towns, insert unrealistic densities, or place an unattainable percentage of regional growth in urban centers. Our urban centers will grow strong if their suburban areas deliver transit riders to the downtown – and if their infill development favors the pedestrian.

To accomplish such a re-balancing, the metropolitan circulation framework should be layered, providing an arterial grid for through auto traffic, neighborhood streets for pedestrians and slow cars, a transit system reinforced by intensified stations, and a pedestrian-dominated urban center. Pockets of mixed-use development with moderate densities and streets designed for both pedestrians and cars would support transit, even in the suburbs. A network of such developments would focus the now sprawling suburban environment, draw traffic from overloaded arterials and freeways, and balance the housing and job opportunities throughout the region.

Affordable Communities and Affordable Housing

The environmental and economic limits of our current pattern of growth are apparent on many levels. The true costs of air pollution, squandered energy, overtaxed resources, and lost open space may be delayed but never fully avoided. The high cost of wasteful energy uses, to mention one of the most serious, runs through our economy and foreign policy. But even leaving aside the long-term environmental impacts of sprawl, the economics of our current development patterns cannot be sustained. The soaring costs of services, infrastructure, road improvements, land, and housing all raise questions about the viability of a land use pattern which has become dysfunctional. The costs of sprawl cannot be met by the average new home buyer, by local governments, or by the environment.

In addition to the public and environmental costs of our auto-dependent communities are high individual, household and personal costs. In the average American household 20 percent of the total budget is spent on transportation. This average does not include, of course, the increasing burden of time lost to commute distances and congestion. The bill helps to bankrupt homebuyers when the price of road maintenance, improvements, and construction, as well as costs for auto storage, are added through development fees to the cost of new housing. Finally, deferred environmental impacts (air quality, lost agricultural lands, habitat, and open space) are just beginning, through minimal government regulation, to filter into the consumer's checkbook. Such government regulations, which adds the costs of environmental impacts now unexpressed in the marketplace, are seen as creating undue burdens to business and consumer. But the resolution to these long-term environmental costs may not have to be increased current costs; it may simply involve a change to more efficient and benign ways of doing things. But, such adjustments are unlikely as long as the true costs remain hidden.

Patterns of development should be judged by life-cycle cost analysis, not just first costs. Life-cycle analysis not only values the present expenditures of a system, building, or institution, but factors in its long term maintenance, resource supply, replacement expense, and clean up and demolition cost. When these currently "external" expenses are included many current investments, such as nuclear power, make little sense. Conversely, many items not economically feasible in a short payback period become quite competitive in a longer time frame once environmental, energy, and

maintenance costs are calculated. Street trees, for example, are considered too expensive for many entry-level subdivisions in the newer parts of Sacramento. In the long term these trees can save significantly in air conditioning bills. The older tree-shaded parts of town are typically ten degrees cooler in the summer than the new treeless suburbs. Although the private marketplace often cannot make such long-term and inclusive judgments, the public sector must begin to demand this broader perspective in setting its criteria for long-term infrastructure investments. Land use patterns, transit systems, solid-waste technologies, water treatment, and even recreation and schools should be seen in this light.

An ecological urban pattern will be economically sound, and a truly economic metropolitan structure will be ecological. Communities in which families are close to shops, jobs, and services will provide a more afford-able lifestyle and therefore a more competitive local economy. Such communities will also decrease costs for local governments, and reduce impacts on the environment. A recent study by Rutgers University comparing compact development to sprawl found that $1.38 billion could be saved in roads, infrastructure, and school construction in New Jersey over the next twenty years. It also found that auto use and air pollution would be significantly reduced and 30,000 acres of farmland would be saved.

All over the country, jobs and businesses migrate to regions with affordable housing, functioning transportation systems, and fiscally sound governmental services. In California, the Central Valley is benefiting from a mass influx from the expensive and congested coastal cities. The challenge for this and similar areas is to prevent a repetition of what occurred in Los Angeles and the Bay Area. As in the New Jersey study, a more compact, mixed-use urban form is critical to the dynamic of ecology and economy.

The need for affordable housing illustrates the desirability of integrated solutions. Strategies for creating affordable housing often run toward subsidies, density bonuses, special financing, and lower construction quality. But subsidies are scarce, multi-family density is an anathema to many neighborhoods, creative financing a rarity in the post-s&l debacle, and construction quality is already cut to the bone. Solutions can no longer come only from the mindset of cutbacks and subsidies. A broader picture of how we form communities and how we see the home itself is central to rethinking this relentless problem.

Affordable housing must start with affordable neighborhoods. Imagine a neighborhood in which transit was within three blocks and ran conveniently every ten minutes. One could stop on a short walk at a daycare center, shops, bank, health club, or video shop. Imagine that the streets were treelined, free of backyard soundwalls, and speeding cars – a neighborhood in which some trips could be made conveniently on foot, transit, or bike. Think of a neighborhood in which a three-car home could be a two-car family, or a two-car home might choose to have only one. Imagine a place in which the average auto miles per household could be 15,000 rather than the average of new suburbs – 30,000 miles per year. A neighborhood in which the money spent on those miles and that car could be used instead for mortgage or rent. And the time spent in the car could be traded for time in the community, with the family, or reading on the train.

Such an walkable neighborhood could support a different type of affordable housing. Take the standard 65' by 100' lot typical in many suburbs and cut it in half, and add an alley and an in-law unit over the garage in the rear. The cost of half a lot will not necessarily be half-price. Finished-lot pricing is part land, streets, and utilities (which is proportional to size) and part services (which is proportional to the number of units). But the lot price per home will be considerably less than full price. The density will be higher – good for transit and local stores – but it will still be a single-family neighborhood – providing the privacy and ownership desired by many. The in-law unit may be used for a relative, a guest, a home office, or a grown child, or it may be used to generate income. In all cases the neighborhood becomes more diverse, more complex, and perhaps more interesting.

The economics of combining these elements – reduced auto costs, small lots, and rental unit income – is instructive. The Sacramento Region represents a good example of the economic conditions in an average mid-sized American metropolis. It has a current population of 1.5 million which is expected to increase by fifty percent in the next twenty years. The cost of owning and operating the average car in the Sacramento area is about $5,000 per year ($415 per month). The cost for an average suburban lot is $60,000. Assume the half-lot is priced at $40,000, a savings of $20,000, and that an in-law unit is affordable housing for a single

BUNGALOW WITH ANCILLARY UNIT

person and brings in $300 per month after tax and costs an additional $15,000 in purchase price. Such a home on a small lot with an in-law unit – in a walkable transit-served neighborhood – sells for $140,000. The mortgage for such a home would be close to $1000. Given the rental income and potential savings on auto ownership or usage, $700 of the monthly mortgage would be covered. We simply turn the people who cannot afford a home into landlords who walk more and the affordable ownership housing problem disappears for those with a down payment. Simultaneously we could create affordable rental housing for singles which is integrated within a diverse, mixed-use community.

Is such a community possible? Typically not. Zoning regulations and the general plans for most cities wouldn't allow the mixed use or the small walkable streets. And they often zone only for single-family or multi-family densities, with nothing as complex as the small-lot home with in-law unit allowed. And finally (since we spend less on mass transit in this country than on advertising cars each year) we don't have transit service convenient enough to justify the savings in auto use, even if we had walkable neighborhoods.

The simplicity of this type of affordable housing is largely unfeasible because of public sector policies rather than economic limits. We choose to subsidize highways rather than transit, we choose to zone mixed-use neighborhoods out of existence, and we choose to standardize and isolate housing types into two large categories: low-density unaffordable or high-density undesirable. Changing these policies will not only begin to resolve some dimensions of the housing question, but can also break the logjam of traffic congestion, deteriorating air quality, and loss of open space. These are simple solutions for complex interconnected problems.

A Taxonomy of Growth

People argue heatedly about growth: where, how much, what type, what density, and if it is really necessary at all. Sprawl is bad, infill is good (if it is not in our neighborhood), new towns destroy open space, master planned communities are sterile, and urban redevelopment is fine for "other people." A region with a high growth demand has several fundamental growth choices: try to limit overall growth; let the towns and suburbs surrounding the metropolitan center grow until they become a continuous mass; attempt to accommodate growth in redevelopment and infill locations; or plan new towns and new growth areas within reasonable transit proximity of the city center. While each strategy has inherent advantages and problems, every region will have to find an appropriate mix of these very different forms of growth.

Limiting growth on a local level without regional controls often spreads development into remote areas more receptive to piecemeal projects. This increases commuting distances and creates our well known hopscotch land use patterns. Sometimes called "Managed" or "Slow" growth, this strategy is often used by a jurisdiction seeking to avoid its fair share of affordable housing or the expansion of transit in its area. Unless there is a strategy for limiting growth at a regional level, local attempts will only extend and displace the problem.

At the other extreme, allowing the uncontrolled growth of existing suburbs and towns is our most common growth strategy. It has the most common results: sprawl, traffic, and a loss of the identity for what may have been distinct neighborhoods, villages, and towns. And it is an approach which seems inevitably to lead to powerful citizens' no-growth movements, growth limitations, and the regional sprawl cited above.

Infill and redevelopment should always be a central part of a region's growth policy. It represents the best utilization of our existing infrastructure and the best opportunity to preserve open space. But to expect infill sites to absorb most new development is often unrealistic, in some cases because there are too few sites to accommodate the demand, and in others because no-growth neighborhood groups inhibit development of infill sites. Once again, without a regional political force to balance the larger economic and environmental needs against the anti-infill tendency of individual communities, there is little hope infill will reach its potential.

There are two general types of infill sites, urban and suburban, and associated with each are special concerns and constraints. Over the last thirty years, urban infill and redevelopment has been a frustrated, but prime, objective for most cities. There have been some successes but many failures. The list of problems is long: racial tensions, economic stagnation, gentrification, ossifying bureaucracy, cheap suburban alternatives, deteriorating schools, and red-line appraisals, to name a few. There are many strategies for resolving or reducing the magnitude of these constraints, and they all need to brought to bear in any future urban infill efforts. But it is clear these strategies are falling short and that additional means to advance urban infill are needed.

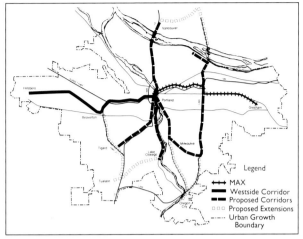

PORTLAND REGIONAL LIGHT RAIL SYSTEM

Portland is an example of a city and region which has gone beyond the traditional programs for infill and urban revitalization. It has successfully supported urban infill in two progressive ways: an Urban Growth Boundary (UGB) and zoning that supports a transit system focused on the central city. The UGB is a state-mandated limit to growth around the metropolitian region which was established in 1972. Both strategies are central to the thesis of this book – that a regional system of open space and transit complemented with development patterns which are pedestrian-friendly can help to re-vitalized an urban center at the same time they order suburban growth. Downtown Portland, because of its light rail transit mall, sensitive urban planning, and regional limits, is growing in a healthy proportion to its suburbs. Jobs in the central business district are expected to grow twenty percent by the year 2010 and account for half of all employment in the region. A site on the light rail line in the downtown recently captured a major regional shopping center. A good example of appropriate infill, the design of this retail center respects and reinforces the traditional urban fabric of Portland, rather than interrupting its pedestrian-scaled city blocks with a typical mall configuration. Both the Urban Growth Boundary and Portland's expanding light rail system has helped to focus new development and economic activity back in its thriving downtown.

Suburban infill represents a different set of prob-lems and constraints. Typically, no-growth and slow-growth neighborhood groups inhibit density and mixed-use while driving the cost of development ever upward. The existing street systems and zoning codes stand as further blocks to creating walkable communi-ties. Finally, the density and configurations typical to suburbia make transit a heavily subsidized safety net rather than a functional alternative to the car. If we are to have significant growth as suburban infill, much must change. Foremost, local citizens must understand that there are options beyond no-growth or sprawl. Local concerns must be tempered with regional needs – needs for an equitable distribution of affordable housing and jobs, needs to preserve open space and agricultural lands, and needs to support transit. This calls for regional poli-cies and governance which can both educate and guide the complex interaction of economics, ecology, juris-diction, and social equity. Unfortunately, suburban infill options may be caught between regional interests and local fears for some time to come.

When urban and suburban infill cannot match the quantity or rate of growth in a region, new growth areas and new towns should be considered. These two forms differ primarily in scale, with the larger new towns incorporating more jobs than new growth areas. Such new growth areas and new towns, if transit-oriented, can complement urban infill. An effective transit sys-tem can help invigorate downtown, as transit envitably focuses on the central business district. Transit deliv-ers people (not just cars) to the heart of our cities, reduces the need for parking structures, and avoids the need for destructive urban freeway projects. Adding more sprawling suburbs to a metropolitan area, in contrast, only increases pressure for more parking and freeways downtown while competing with the city for jobs and retail activity. Adding transit-oriented new towns and new growth areas can reinforce the city's role as the region's cultural and economic center. The transit sys-tem that is supported at the region's edge with new growth can also become the catalyst for redevelopment and infill at the center.

The recent history of new towns and new growth areas, sometimes called master planned communities, has given such developments a bad name. In Europe, with some notable exceptions, new towns are sterile and suburban. In America they are sterile, suburban, and, even worse, economic failures – for at least the first 20 years. But the question remains: are these qualities inherent or a product of a dysfunctional design philosophy? And if new towns could be designed more intelligently, would they be justified or necessary?

To answer this question it is useful to understand the history of new town planning. At the turn of the century and during the great depression the theory of new towns evolved in several directions. Ebenezer Howard and the Garden Cities movement defined a Luddite's vision of small towns built for workers surrounded by a greenbelt, combining the best of city and country. These towns were formed around rail stations and formally configured with a combination of the Romantic and Beaux Arts urban traditions; powerful civic spaces surrounded by village-scaled neighborhoods. In the same period Tony Garnier developed the first modernist approach to town planning, segregating industry, isolating different uses, and freeing buildings from the street. His was the first modernist vision of the twentieth-century city. During the depression Le Corbusier and Frank Lloyd Wright expanded this modernist vision in the urban and suburban context while retaining fundamental modernist principles: segregation of use, love of the auto, and dominance of private over public space. In these utopias (which after WWII came to guide development patterns) the street as the community's habitable common ground disintegrated. Even in the most progressive of the post-WWII new towns and master planned communities, these basic modernist postulates have compromised, if not destroyed, their ability to evolve into vital urban communities. The next generation of new towns should learn from these failures, avoiding their sterile and suburban character while defining a form of growth that can help mend the metropolis.

It is often hard to pin down the difference between new growth

WELWYN GARDEN CITY,
EBENEZER HOWARD & LOUIS SOISSONS

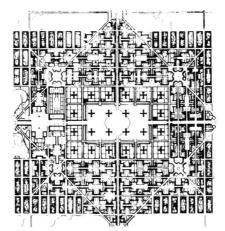

CONTEMPORARY CITY,
LE CORBUSIER

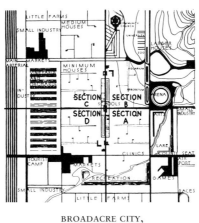

BROADACRE CITY,
FRANK LLOYD WRIGHT

areas: suburb, "edge city" or "new town." Suburbs have become more like Modernist new towns; they have jobs, retail, recreation, and a diverse population. They also have their placeless quality. And when you study the planning procedures required of suburban "master planned communities" and "specific area plans," they resemble intentional new towns in scale, effort, and conception. But neither are real towns and probably never will be. Suburbs lack, as do many of the so-called modern new towns and "Edge Cities," the fundamental qualities of real towns: pedestrian scale, an identifiable center and edge, integrated diversity of use and population, and defined public space.

These qualities are lacking in our growth patterns regardless of context. Urban infill sites, suburban new development areas, master planned communities, and new towns all fail when planned without pedestrian scale, land use diversity, public space, and a strong center. Urban infill often succeeds because these qualities pre-exist and need only be preserved, not necessarily created. Nevertheless we see many infill projects which succeed in destroying these pre-existing qualities. Modern suburbs and new towns clearly lack a real center, definitive edges, or significant common ground. They have diversity in use and user, but these diverse elements are segregated by the car. They have none of the places for casual and spontaneous interaction which create vital neighborhoods, quarters, or towns. In short they are without pedestrian scale.

In every context the quality of new development should follow town-like principles: housing for a diverse population, a full mix of uses, walkable streets, positive public space, integrated civic and commercial centers, transit orientation, and accessible open space. For urban infill, such development can become "new town in town" designs. For smaller parcels in existing urban neighborhoods the task is to complete the mix of a community while honoring the unique qualities of the place. For suburban sites, even with the political constraints, mixed-use neighborhoods can be infilled. No blank slate, suburban infill sites sometimes offer rich histories to work with, as well as debilitating sprawl to overcome.

Satellite new towns at the outer edge of the metropolitan region can help provide greenbelts for the region. At the same time they buffer their own edges, they can help establish permanent edges for the region. Without greenbelted new towns or stable Urban Growth Boundaries, a fast-growing region will continually expand into close-in natural edges and open space. Additionally, new towns can help manage the growth of older suburbs and towns by absorbing excess development demand and permanently positioning their open space buffers.

Sprawl is destructive in all conditions – as infill, suburban growth, or new towns. Projects which are diverse, centered, and walkable are useful in all three areas. The specific nature of a metropolitan region will dictate how many and which of these growth strategies are necessary and useful. Some regions with a very slow rate of growth may only need incremental infill. Some regions with fast growth and much undeveloped suburban land may benefit from both infill and new growth area projects. Other regions may require all three strategies, including new towns, to absorb massive growth without destroying the identity of existing small towns and urban centers. The quality of development we allow, not just its location or size, is the principal problem and opportunity of growth.

Integrated Regional Planning and Political Will

Along with piecemeal land use planning at the local level, we have piecemeal planning at the state and federal level. The problems of open space preservation, affordable housing, highway congestion, air quality, and infrastructure costs are treated independently at these levels, as if there were no linkages. Policy makers have persisted in unsuccessfully treating only the symptoms of these integrated problems rather than addressing the development patterns at their root. We control air pollution with tailpipe emissions, fuel consumption with more efficient engines, and congestion with more freeways, rather than simply making cities and towns in which people are less auto-dependent. Treating both symptom and cause is now essential for real and meaningful change.

At the federal level, public investment in roads, transit, housing, civic facilities, and open space must be tied to more efficient and sustainable patterns of community development. But these patterns of community development cannot be realized by localized growth control measures or discontinuous jurisdictions. Progressive federal and state policies must be administered by regional governance to intelligently guide development and our larger investments.

The absence of long-term regional policies results in development patterns which do not adequately consider the overall environmental or economic implications of piecemeal growth. The problem is multifaceted: first, local land use control is balkanized and unable to balance the regional issues of jobs/housing distribution, transit, air quality, traffic, and open space; second, current land use controls are outmoded, responding to outdated conditions with outdated strategies; and third, federal policies and investments redirect growth unconsciously and fail to integrate the problems. People are fed up with sprawl, but rather than comprehensive regional planning we see a rising tide of building moratoriums and down-zoning. The result is a policy gridlock in which development is endlessly delayed and diluted – adding cost but not quality to growth.

Without a land use policy reform strategy, Congress, state legislatures, and local jurisdictions will continue to be limited to treating the symptoms of socially harmful development patterns, instead of addressing the cause. For example, fuel consumption is largely a result of sprawling land use patterns that compel use of the car. Congress has attempted to cut fuel consumption by increasing the fuel efficiency of cars. The new car fleet went from 13 mpg in 1973 to 29 mpg in 1989. Yet even this impressive doubling of fuel efficiency was outstripped by the continuing explosion of sprawl-driven auto use: the U. S. transportation sector burned 19 percent more fuel in 1989 than in 1973. In the last twenty years, while the California population increased by 40 percent, the vehicle miles traveled have increased by 100 percent. We are driving more and we (and the environment) are enjoying it less. But the form of our communities gives us few viable alternatives.

Air pollution is another symptom of sprawl which cannot be cured without treating the disease itself. The 1990 amendments to the Clean Air Act are predicted to cut carbon monoxide, nitrous oxide, and hydrocarbons by 10% by the year 2000. However, despite the tightened tailpipe emission standards, sprawl-induced increases are projected to make these same pollutants 30% worse in 2010 than they were in 1989.

Highway congestion results from the trips generated by poor land use decisions. Yet solving congestion by building more freeways is self-defeating as well as ineffective. New roads and road improvements in existing developed areas are sorely needed. While adding new freeways and beltways may temporarily reduce congestion, it does nothing to reduce trips, and often increases auto use by inducing more sprawl. Apart from that, the money available to deficit-strapped federal and state legislative bodies is inadequate to build freeways fast enough to keep up with traffic growth, even assuming freeways had no other problems.

Even though treating only the symptoms is clearly inadequate, addressing the land use question at the root raises many legitimate concerns. Changing land use patterns is a monumental task, and it is fair to question the viability and effectiveness of such an approach.

The land planning principles of Transit-Oriented Development have now been developed and tested in several major regions across the U.S: San Diego, Sacramento, Portland, and Montgomery County, Maryland. While there are few fully functioning models of this approach to development, studies show that households in older neighborhoods, which share many of the prime characteristics of Transit-Oriented Development, travel half the auto miles per year when compared to households in a modern suburb. These older neighborhoods are mixed-use, walkable, and have adequate transit services. Similar studies document a quadrupling of transit use and a doubling of walking and biking in these older neighborhoods. The highway congestion, fuel consumption, and air quality implications are plain.

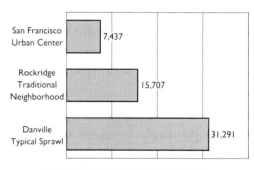

VEHICLE MILES TRAVELED PER YEAR

It is time to break the cycle of government investment in an "interstate system" of highways which fundamentally breeds sprawl on the beltways of our cities while subsidizing decentralization. Our efforts to improve air quality, preserve sensitive habitat, open space, and agricultural lands, provide affordable housing and lifestyles, and reduce congestion are constantly contradicted by the land use patterns indirectly supported by these highway investments. Coherent land use patterns should guide our public investments in roads, infrastructure, open space, and transit. In fact, such investments ought to be made contingent on redirecting the growth in our regions toward more compact, affordable, walkable, and transit-oriented forms.

Such a major reordering of government policies and subsidies will take a powerful political coalition. The coalition against such integrated planning can be large: localities looking for growth and tax base regardless of development quality or regional implications; developers looking for opportunities to repeat past successes without regard for changing times or consequences; neighborhood groups hoping to preserve and enhance property values by exclusionary practices; and people (i.e. voters) simply afraid of the unknown or a loss of control. The forces for the status quo are powerful drives that are self-reinforcing. The defensive desire for a secure and exclusive private domain, and the tendency of specialists to maximize segments rather than wholes, both conspire to inhibit change.

The multi-faceted dimensions of the problems facing the American metropolis could form the foundation of an alliance between environmentalists, developers, and urban advocates. Environmentalists increasingly recognize that we must selectively build our way out of land use problems. Preserving open space while supporting a growing transit system should be basic goals for the environmental community. This means encouraging housing and jobs to be built in concert with transit investments rather than simply opposing sprawl. Housing and jobs linked to transit should be as much a part of an environmental agenda as pollution controls or open space conservation.

Those that advocate inner-city investments ought to support regional transit systems and Urban Growth Boundaries as part of their strategy to get housing and commercial development in central city locations. Inner-city investment gains a broader rationale when joined with proposals for regional transportation and open-space systems. By linking the two objectives, and by transcending the urban/suburban boundary, both environmentalists and urban reformers gain allies. Green space should be part of the transit-oriented development concept of regional infrastructure investment, along with inner-city redevelopment.

The private sector also can become an ally in this strategy. The development community needs financing for infrastructure expansion and a dependable road map of land use policy. Current conditions force them into years of expensive, lengthy, and uncertain approval process. Because many municipalities are unable to fully fund services and infrastructure, fees are disproportionately added to developments to cover what was once a more efficient and evenly distributed public burden. Regional plans that provide certainty and expedient entitlements would be a boon to the development industry. And more compact, infrastructure-efficient development patterns would further reduce costs.

But ultimately, the development community must respond to the marketplace, providing what the home buyer or business seeks. Mixed-use, walkable, and transit-served developments are gaining broad acceptance in a market wise to the shortcomings of stand-alone office parks, subdivisions and shopping malls. This market acceptance is in some sense a signal that many now perceive the problems and understand that more of the same will not work.

These three constituencies – environmentalists, enlightened developers, and inner-city advocates – can find common purpose in regional planning goals. They can form a powerful coalition for larger scale ecological programs, expedited permit processing, efficient and affordable housing polices, and regional investments that balance inner-city needs with regional growth. Each share a concern for the next generation – those who cannot be in the voting booth today. The developers because they would like to build for them, the environmentalists because they seek to preserve healthy ecosystems for them, and the urbanists because they hope to pass on a more equitable and stable society.

APPLE COMPUTER LOCATED AT MIXED-USE LAGUNA WEST OVER MANY TYPICAL OFFICE PARKS

Public Poverty and Private Affluence

In the same way that the metropolis is a mirror of the American Dream, government and its policies are a mirror of our social character. The rise of the modern suburb is in part a manifestation of a deep cultural and political shift away from public life. Such an inclination has certainly been a part of our society for some time. But historically a secure private domain complemented a rich public world. It did not displace it.

The balance between a secluded, segregated private life and a diverse, shared public life has changed dramatically in recent decades. The suburbs have come to represent and facilitate the privatization of our lives in social form, in political priorites, and in physical character. The movement is circular; the more privatized our technology and social forms become, the more isolated and defensive we are. To walk or take transit is a public act which makes the street a safer component of community; to drive is a private act which turns the street into a utility. The former leads in many ways to a richer public domain, the latter to the world we have come to know, if not love. The loss of variety in these modes is both the symbol and the reality of a loss of balance between our private and public lives.

The gated community is perhaps the most blatant and literal expression of the trend. Physically it denotes the separation, and sadly the fear, that has become the subtext of a country once founded on differences and tolerance. Politically it expresses the desire to privatize, cutting back the responsibilities of government to provide services for all and replacing it with private and focused institutions: private schools, private recreation, private parks, private roads, even quasi-private governments. Socially, the house fortress represents a self-fulfilling prophecy. The more isolated people become and the less they share with others unlike themselves, the more they *do* have to fear. To this extent privatization is a powerful force in the marketplace which directs the home-building industry and our land use patterns.

The private domain, whether in a car, a home, or a subdivision, sets the direction of the modern suburb. But it is a direction affordable to a rapidly decreasing segment of the culture. It may be that more open, integrated communities could be built for people desirous of a more public life. For many others, such a shift may be their only economic choice. Perhaps this constraint can become a virtue by necessity. Or it may be creating a different kind of self-fulfilling prophecy; the more diverse and open a community is, the less people come to fear one another. There are may unknowns about this direction, but the argument is central to viability of the American Metropolis as it is described in this book. In fact, one of the primary obstacles to innovations in community planning remains the impulse toward a more gated and private world.

Consider the kinds of people who may freely choose or profit from a more integrated, walkable community. Kids certainly thrive in neighborhoods where they can get around on their own. Once many believed that the subdivision offered the protected domain children need. But it is increasingly clear that it offers too little access, with parents shuffling them around to scheduled activities, rather than enabling kids to make their own worlds and events. Additionally, the many dangers subdivisions hoped to exclude now follow kids into their schools, their hangouts, and even the once secluded cul-de-sac.

Working parents certainly could also profit from a less isolated lifestyle. Mixed-use neighborhoods become more convenient because the demands on adults to be chauffeurs could be reduced and daily needs brought closer. Working women clearly have much to gain from such circumstances. They are too often the ones called upon to link all the pieces now dispersed in suburbia. The elderly also might choose the life of a "town-like" place over the suburb, given the chance to do so. Walkable places with interesting activities and services might extend their independence. Singles have always gravitated to places that offer a rich public life. And there are others, across demographic lines, who simply desire a richer public experience and a stronger sense of community.

The reality, of course, is that both impulses reside in all of us: a defensive exclusionary desire for retreat and an optimistic desire to create community. Many factors play in the balance between these universal impulses, including history, traditions, technology, ideology, environment, subsidies and economic necessity to name a few. Our history and traditions offer much to support both. The nature of our current technologies, from cars and TVs to computers and VCRs, clearly facilitate a retreat into the private domain. New economic pressures, in the largest sense, will now move us back toward stronger communities and more environmentally benign technologies. But the choice we make is finally personal and complex, drawing on our values, our aesthetics, and finally our optimism. The beauty of our culture is that experiments will happen. Through this experimentation new directions will be found that express the complex interactions between our patterns of settlement and our lives.

GUIDELINES

The following guidelines define an integrated strategy for growth in our cities, suburbs, and towns. Unlike typical "design guidelines," which deal primarily with aesthetic and architectural principles, these guidelines attempt to define a new context and direction for the built environment – for the way we develop our communities, neighborhoods, districts, and regions. They are shaped according to three general principles: first, that the regional structure of growth should be guided by the expansion of transit and a more compact urban form; second, that our ubiquitous single-use zoning should be replaced with standards for mixed-use, walkable neighborhoods; and third, that our urban design policies should create an architecture oriented toward the public domain and human dimension rather than the private domain and auto scale.

Technically the guidelines can operate at different scales. They can be used to redirect and reconfigure a region's General or Comprehensive Plans, help establish Urban Growth Boundaries, designate appropriate new growth and infill areas, aid in setting standards for the development or redevelopment of neighborhoods through "Specific Area Plans," and they can help to revise existing zoning ordinances to allow more mixed-use, pedestrian-oriented land plans.

The Transit-Oriented Development (TOD) concept is simple: moderate and high-density housing, along with complementary public uses, jobs, retail and services, are concentrated in mixed-use developments at strategic points along the regional transit system. Recently, similar concepts have gone by many names: Pedestrian Pockets, Traditional Neighborhood Developments, Urban Villages, and Compact Communities to name a few. Although different in detail and emphasis, these concepts share a common perspective, design principles, and set of goals. TODs add emphasis to the integration of transit on a regional basis, providing a perspective missing from strategies which deal primarily with the nature and structure of individual communities and neighborhoods. This regional perspective helps to define a meaningful edge for the metropolitan area, eliminating the danger of random growth in distant sites served only by highways. Such a larger view can help order growth across our balkanized metropolitan regions as well as encourage infill and redevelopment efforts. Transit is not the only goal of these development patterns, it is however a potential end result which adds to a strategy with many other benefits.

A "walkable" environment is perhaps the key aspect of the concept. In order to develop alternatives to drive-alone auto use, comfortable pedestrian environments should be created at the origin and destination of each trip. No one likes to arrive at work without a car if they cannot walk comfortably from transit to their destination or run a mid-day errand on foot. TODs seek to bring many destinations within walking distance, allowing trips to be combined. Placing local retail, parks, day care, civic services, and transit at the center of a TOD reinforces the opportunity to walk or bike for many errands, as well as combine a trip to transit with other stops. Streets lined by trees and building entries also help to make the TOD environment "pedestrian-friendly." Although focused on reinforcing transit, such land use configurations would equally support carpools and more efficient auto use. Given historic development trends and projections for the future, each of these travel modes can play an important role in solving a city's or region's increasing traffic problems.

Transit-Oriented Developments can, and ironically should, develop without transit – with a justifiable focus on the pedestrian and a healthier community structure. More walkable, integrated communities can help relieve our dependence on the auto in many ways other than just transit. Reducing trip lengths, combining destinations, carpooling, walking, and biking are all enhanced by TODs. A healthy walking environment can succeed without transit, but a transit system cannot exist without the pedestrian. The growth of such pedestrian-friendly developments, if coordinated at a regional scale, can form the armature for future transit growth. In fact, this type of development must precede, not just follow, the growth of our transit networks. TODs can exist without transit, but our transit systems have little chance of surviving in the low-density environment of sprawling suburbs without TODs.

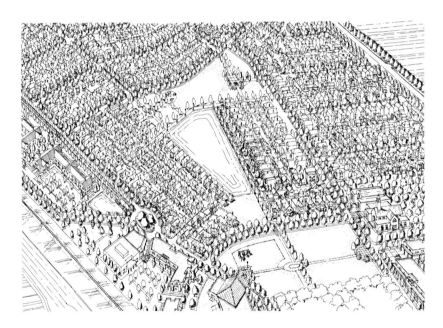

The fundamental structure of the TOD is nodal – focused on a commercial center, civic uses, and a potential transit stop. This nodal quality is the result of the contemporary bias of retail to develop in distinct "packages," the spacing requirements of transit stations, and the qualitative need for an identifiable social center in our neighborhoods and districts. This is in sharp contrast to the linear form which used to dominate the form of grid towns or strip commercial suburbs. Defined by a comfortable walking distance, the TOD is made up of a core commercial area, with civic and transit uses integrated, and a flexible program of housing, jobs, and public space surrounding it. The densities and mix of these primary uses, though controlled by certain minimums, is determined by the specifics of each site and economy. Surrounding the TOD is a Secondary Area for low-density uses, the large-lot single-family residences, schools, larger businesses, and major parks.

There are many "mixed-use" Planned Unit Developments and Master Planned Communities which speak of similar goals but employ fundamentally different planning principles. These strategies, which have dominated the "progressive" side of sprawl for some time now, differ from TODs in several significant ways.

First, while they typically have a mix of uses, they unfortunately separate these uses into individual development zones segregated by major arterial roadways and property lines. This segregation often makes walkable connections weak. Second, they tend to isolate the pedestrian from the street, either on greenways or designated paths, leaving the street solely for auto use. Third, they still employ a hierarchy of streets, focusing congestion by forcing traffic onto the arterial network. Fourth, they continue to design neighborhood streets for the convenience and speed of autos rather than for a mix of uses and slower traffic. And finally, they reverse the hierarchy of public and private space by facilitating an architecture of autonomous "objects" rather than an architecture which helps define and create memorable public places.

TODs not only promote alternates to auto use, but can be a formula for affordable communities – affordable in many senses. Communities are affordable to the environment when they efficiently use land, help to preserve open space, and reduce air pollution; they are affordable for diverse households when a variety of housing types, at various costs and densities, are encouraged in convenient locations; they are affordable to families with limited incomes when the mix and configuration of uses allow reduced auto dependence and auto-related expenses; they are affordable to businesses seeking to relocate when the workforce can be freed of the gridlock and high housing costs typical in many growing metropolitan regions; and they are affordable to the public taxpayer when infrastructure is efficient, and public amenities are well-used.

In summary, the principles of Transit-Oriented Development are to:

- organize growth on a regional level to be compact and transit-supportive;

- place commercial, housing, jobs, parks, and civic uses within walking distance of transit stops;

- create pedestrian-friendly street networks which directly connect local destinations;

- provide a mix of housing types, densities, and costs;

- preserve sensitive habitat, riparian zones, and high quality open space;

- make public spaces the focus of building orientation and neighborhood activity; and

- encourage infill and redevelopment along transit corridors within existing neighborhoods.

These principles are not new; they are simply a return to the timeless goals of urbanism, in its best sense. They are principles which over time have created our most treasured man-made environments and which, although constantly evolving with culture and technology, remain true to the human dimension and our deepest social aspirations. But they are fundamentally different from the ideas that have guided planning for the last two generations.

Sustainable Communities, Pedestrian Pockets, and Transit-Oriented Development

A brief history of the progression of ideas and models which led to the guidelines may be helpful in understanding their underlying assumptions and concepts. The book *Sustainable Communities* was an early work which attempted to redefine our patterns of settlement primarily in relation to environmental concerns.

RADBURN, NJ

Involving biologists, architects, sociologists, traffic engineers, planners, and economists, it was a multidisciplinary effort to show how ecological systems could be integrated into cities, suburbs, and new towns. It succeeded in demonstrating technologies and designs which could build a more ecological infrastructure for communities through energy conservation, waste recycling, open space preservation, and walkable neighborhoods. But in some ways it went too far in literally bringing nature into the human settlement. The balance between urbanism and naturalism was lost – urban vitality was too often sacrificed to green spaces in an effort to incorporate organic systems within the city. The concerns became almost myopic; buildings locked in a single orientation to optimize solar heating, for example. Communities should be compact, diverse, and urban, and their natural systems should be integrated at a regional scale, not necessarily in each block and neighborhood.

A simple expression of this imbalance between urbanism and environmentalism was in the treatment of the street. Separating the pedestrian onto "greenways" and carless paths was a flawed strategy from the Radburn experiment of the 1930s – a neighborhood design which, in attempting to control the car, sacrificed the street to it. Likewise the Modernist's "building in the park" approach to town planning ultimately helped kill the life of the street by separating it from the activities of the buildings that lined it. Both of these approaches were incorrectly adopted into *Sustainable Communities* and the models it presented. Environmentally sound communities need parks, regional greenbelts, and high-quality open space, but they also need density and street-life. Isolated from a larger concept of human habitat, the environmental movement could be in danger of becoming another "special interest group" which can optimize its goals while losing sight of a larger purpose.

Through a grant from the NEA arts program I had an opportunity, along with architect Mark Mack, to develop designs which attempted to integrate environmentalism and urbanism. On the one hand the ideas were greatly influenced by Leon Krier who defined, in his early works, a pure and compelling vision of urbanism. On the other was the problem of the American suburb and the decentralizing forces that produced our current palette of building types. The work became an attempt to join these two seemingly divergent directions.

The concept that resulted used walkable, mixed-use neighborhoods to reinforce transit, preserve open space, and make a more compact metropolitan form. These places, called Pedestrian Pockets, were meant to form a regional network spanning infill and greenfield sites, inner-city and suburban locations. They were built on the notion that retail, employment, and transit were nodal and decentralizing at a rapid rate. The diagram for the Pedestrian Pocket mixed several mid- to high-density housing types with jobs over shops at a transit stop. The size of the Pocket was set by the comfortable walking distance of one quarter mile. Although a grid, it was still based on the Radburn model; cul-de-sac streets with segregated pedestrian paths leading to the center.

Since that time the concepts evolved through theoretical design research at University of California at Berkeley, design charrettes at University of Washington, and through private practice. One of the charrettes produced a book, *The Pedestrian Pocket Book*, which outlined the thinking prior to the practical experience of major regional and neighborhood planning projects. Under the influence of the private sector projects, the design approach was expanded to include a clearer understanding of the development types viable in the current marketplace – the architectural components which could make the concepts buildable today. The realities of the modern American city require a model which incorporates and reconfigures the diverse uses at work in the marketplace, not a theoretical construct which hypothesizes a fundamental change in the architectural "building blocks" of development.

The original Pedestrian Pocket model was expanded through the larger projects to include concepts for new towns, regional growth strategies, and a wider range of residential densities – particularly low-density single-family homes, the mainstay of sprawl. Incorporating a reasonable and realistic proportion of single-family housing called for a fundamental rethinking of a model which started primarily as a multi-family infill proposal. "Secondary Areas" were added around the denser mixed-

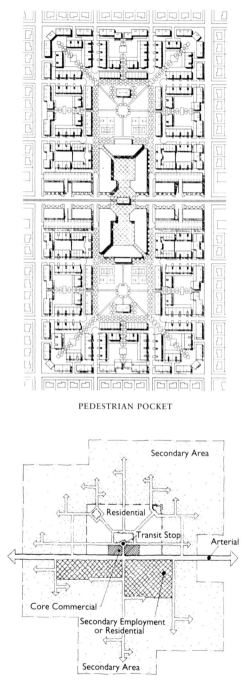

PEDESTRIAN POCKET

TRANSIT-ORIENTED DEVELOPMENT

45

use core to incorporate many of the low intensity uses excluded from the early Pedestrian Pocket model. This provided an excellent location for large schools, major recreation parks, and light industrial uses, as well as a range of single-family housing. The larger projects also fostered consideration of transit and its implications on regional form as well as the structure of individual neighborhoods. They ultimately produced the guidelines for "Transit-Oriented Development" from which this section of the book is derived.

Transit-Oriented Development and Travel Behavior

Central to the utility of these concepts is their implications on travel behavior: the way we choose to get around, the frequency of trips, and the distance of each journey. Though many factors other than land use configurations affect our travel behavior – such as the cost of gas, auto ownership, parking expenses, the amount of time lost to congestion, and the quality of transit – the effects of land use on travel behavior are formative. In fact, land use patterns are the foundation upon which the viability of travel cost, time, and investment factors depend. If land use primarily supports the auto, then increasing the costs of operating cars and allowing congestion to grow will only result in pain, not a fundamental reorientation of travel behavior. Without coordinated land use policies, increasing transit investments will only lead to underutilized facilities. On the other hand, if land use configurations support alternatives to the car, then many results are possible: people may choose to walk, bike, and use transit more often; they can combine trips more easily; there may be shorter, more direct routes to local destinations; they may actually be able to reduce the number of cars they own; and because of these changes, reduced congestion on highways and arterial roadways is possible.

As land use patterns and travel behavior change, many positive "feedbacks" can occur. If transit ridership rises, service can be increased and transit becomes convenient for more people. As air quality improves, health costs could be reduced. As more people walk or use bikes, the federal and local costs for road and highway maintenance can be reduced. With more people arriving at work or shopping areas without their cars, the size of parking lots can be limited. The end result of shifts away from auto usage would result in reduced energy consumption, greenhouse effect, and dependence on foreign oil. But these changes are dependent on understanding, quantifying, and valuing the effect that land use can have on travel behavior. Unfortunately these linkages are not fully understood.

Traffic engineers have developed sophisticated modeling programs for predicting the multiple and interdependent effects of population growth and traffic. The models are calibrated by, and therefore tend to replicate, the way things are in our sprawling cities – rather than the way things could be. These programs are sensitive to household size, household incomes, residential density, costs of travel, congestion levels, type of trips, and proximity of destinations. But they are not sensitive to the walkability of a neighborhood, the density of destinations within a neighborhood (a measure of mixed-use), or the implications of these factors on transit use. They effectively are not sensitive to the possibilities of walkable and transit-oriented communities.

In order to fully understand the dynamic of land use and travel behavior, and be able to use it in the design of communities, the components of traffic analysis must be understood. There are several critical yardsticks used in traffic analysis, each with special implications. Auto ownership per household is a fundamental measure of the travel bias of a region. And it affects the pressed American household budget directly. In California, auto ownership per household has been increasing while the size of households has been falling. Across the country our love affair with the car is becoming more of an obsession when compared to other industrialized countries. In an average Swedish city there are 1.5 autos per household, compared with an average 2.2 autos per household in the USA.

Vehicle Miles Traveled (VMT) per household is another significant milestone. VMT directly affects the amount of road usage and therefore maintenance and construction costs. Once again, VMT has been increasing much faster than the growth in population would predict; from 1969 to 1990 it increased 82 percent while the national population only increased 21 percent.

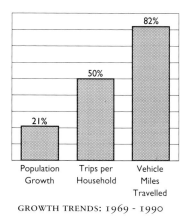

GROWTH TRENDS: 1969 - 1990

The number of trips per household per day is another factor on the rise, from approximately eight per household per day in 1969 to twelve in 1990. Trip generation is critical because it is used to calculate the effect of development on local street intersections and because

air quality is directly related to the number of times a car is started (cold starts) rather than simply the distance traveled.

Finally, "mode split" is the percent of trips by each type of travel means: auto, walking, bike, or transit. It can vary greatly, depending on the quality of the environment and demographics. For example, suburban Huntington Beach has a 91% auto mode split while inner-city Philadelphia has only 23% of all trips in autos. Each of these interdependent travel factors is governed by the type of communities we build and the economics of the alternatives.

Different countries demonstrate significant variations in the relationship between land use, public transportation policies, and travel behavior. In European communities auto use is generally between 30% and 48% of all trips; transit comprises between 11% and 26% of all trips; and pedestrian/bike trips are from 33% to 50% of the total (transit there is supported with healthy pedestrian environments). In comparison, the U.S. average mode split is 86% via auto, 8% walking, 3% bike, and 3% by transit. Canada has a similar walk/bike mode split but a much higher transit utilization – 15% of all trips rather than 3%.

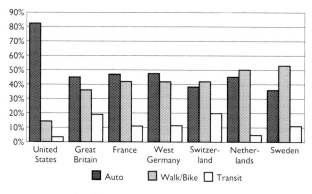

MODE SPLIT AS PERCENT OF TOTAL TRIPS

Of course the cost of gas and transit infrastructure investments affect these distributions, along with land use patterns. In Europe today gas costs are three times those in the USA. Perhaps this explains a portion of the difference. But to what degree are our land use configurations inhibiting our ability to set similar public

47

pricing policies? And to what degree would more compact, walkable, and transit-oriented land use patterns independently change travel behavior?

Although few of the new generation of TODs or Traditional Neighborhoods have matured to a stage to answer these questions directly, neighborhoods with similar characteristics – typically built before WWII – may offer a reasonable comparison. One study by Fehr & Peers Associates for the International Association of Traffic Engineers compared older TOD-like neighborhoods in the San Francisco Bay Area with some of its newer suburban areas. These older neighborhoods were not inner-city locations with high densities, but the older centers of small towns throughout the region. Taken from travel surveys conducted in 1980, the results showed both a significantly lower number of trips per household (nine in the TOD-like neighborhoods vs. eleven in the new suburbs) and a dramatic shift in the mode split. Auto trips were 86% in the suburbs while only 64% in older neighborhoods. Walking and bike trips were 19% for the older neighborhoods and 11% in the suburbs. The transit trips in the older neighborhoods accounted for 17% of the total vs. only 3% in the suburban areas.

A similar survey in Portland, Oregon showed that walking trips in the older, mixed-use neighborhoods were three times those of the typical suburb. In another empirical study done by John Holtzclaw of NRDC in the Bay Area, odometer readings were aggregated by neighborhood type and location. The TOD-like neighborhoods had almost half the VMT per household per year of the new suburbs; 15,700 miles vs. 31,300. Using the cost per mile developed by Hertz Corporation in 1987 of $0.57, this difference represents a savings of $8,883 per year for the average household in a TOD-like neighborhood.

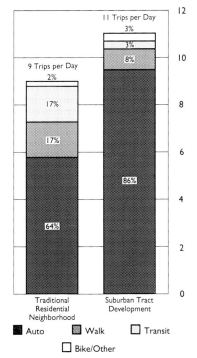

DAILY TRIP GENERATION IN
THE SAN FRANCISCO BAY AREA

There were several factors other than land use configuration which affected this dramatic shift for the older neighborhoods. Lower average household incomes, better transit service, and closer proximity to the metropolitan center all characterized the older neighborhoods. New TODs may not be able to match the proximity and they may have slightly higher average incomes than the older neighborhoods, but they should have equivalent transit service and similar land use diversity and density. Even if new TODs cannot exactly replicate the performance of these older neighborhoods, the numbers indicate a possible range of results that are very promising. And they are, in cultural nature and public policy, specific to America.

It has been shown that a higher percentage of people are likely to use transit if they can walk to the station, rather than get in their cars to drive to a "park-and-ride" lot. As the convenience retail, recreational, civic, and entertainment elements of new TODs develop, combined trips would increase as people run errands on foot to and from the transit stop. Park-and-ride lots would continue to be a part of any transit system, but should not typically be located within TODs. Transit utilization in TODs would increase over time as the mix of uses reaches build-out, as the transit corridor develops, and as residents and employees come to see the convenience of transit service. Simultaneously, the type of transit service coming to TODs can mature. It may start with local bus service, add express bus service as ridership grows, and finally provide fixed rail connections.

Even without increasing transit or walk trips, the TOD street system can reduce traffic congestion on major streets. Standard suburban development patterns presently force all local shopping, recreation, and school trips, as well as work trips, onto the arterial street system.

This pattern leads to the congestion about which neighborhood groups typically are most concerned. In a hypothetical study by Walter Kulash for the American Society of Civil Engineers, a suburb with standard street configurations was compared with a mixed-use development with a grid of local street connections. Because of the more direct routing possible in the gridded neighborhood, the overall VMT for trips with destinations in the area was reduced by 33% and the VMT on the arterial network was reduced by 75%. Although this study only calculates local trips and not through traffic, such local trips typically represent over 50% of all travel. Clearly, an interconnected system of local streets, internal to the neighborhood, reduces congestion on main roads even if people are using their cars. In TODs, arterials are seen as edges, providing for through traffic and regional access only. Local streets should be designed to minimize the potential for through traffic while providing access to local destinations.

Clearly much more research and analysis is needed to clarify and quantify the potential results of a new land use pattern on our travel behavior. It is critical work; critical to effectively directing federal and state transportation dollars, critical to many of our most pressing environmental issues, and critical to our quality of life. We are driving twice as much as we did in the 1970s yet the result seems to be less mobility and more frustration. Understanding this important linkage is fundamental to charting an intelligent and benign vision of the Next American Metropolis.

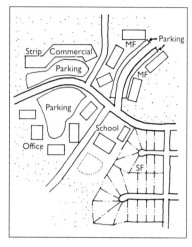

CONVENTIONAL SUBURBAN
DEVELOPMENT

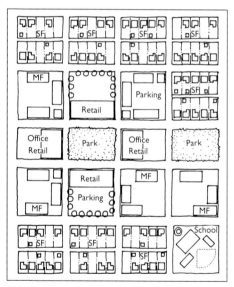

TRADITIONAL NEIGHBORHOOD DEVELOPMENT

49

Regional Context and Implementation

Where and how these guidelines are used is critical to their success. The overall distribution of development rights across three primary types of sites – redevelopment, infill, and new growth areas – must be balanced and analyzed from a regional perspective; balanced in environmental, economic, and social terms. The quantity and limitations of infill and redevelopment sites must be understood when making decisions on the quantity and location of new growth areas. In the reverse, too many new growth areas may reduce demand for inner-city redevelopment and infill. The balance is complex and critical; on the one hand economic health for the region often calls for suburban housing opportunities and adequate industrial sites, on the other hand too much of such growth can drain investment from the city. Regional land use governance is key to applying these land use patterns in a way which creates viable transit systems, open space networks, and inner-city reinvestment as well as a vital regional economy. In each of the potential settings, Redevelopment, Infill, and New Growth areas, TOD plans should respond to sensitive environmental circumstances and to the context and character of existing adjacent neighborhoods.

Inner-city development has been a crucial problem for most regions; a problem with many dimensions. Planning at a regional scale, with transit expansion as a framework, can play a role in focusing development into these critical areas. Using the catalyst of transit and redevelopment funding, inner-city areas and older neighborhoods may gradually transition to new and more intensive uses. Such changes should be guided to reinforce the transit system, producing land uses and configurations that are more pedestrian-oriented, affordable, and linked to the greater metropolitan region. Intensification and redevelopment must, however, be balanced with sensitivity to protecting existing neighborhoods and a recognition that additional development is not appropriate in every setting.

Infill sites, land that has been "skipped over" but is surrounded by existing development, often occur in areas similar to redevelopable sites. However, infill sites are often large enough to develop all or a major portion of a TOD, with the existing surrounding neighborhoods functioning as a support area. Both infill and redevelopment sites can be located in older urban areas or in new suburban situations. When a street grid is present, as is typical in older inner-city locations, horizontal connections between local uses is easy and small sites can develop to balance the mix of uses surrounding it. In the new suburban context the disconnected street patterns make it difficult to establish walkable connections to local destinations. Therefore smaller infill opportunities cannot simply add a missing component to the neighborhood, they must also provide the walkable connections. One prime infill and redevelopment possibility exists in the suburban fabric: old commercial areas with large parking lots offer the opportunity to insert density and new uses into central suburban locations.

Finally, each metropolitan region has viable New Growth Areas which are environmentally suitable for development and are within reasonable distance of transit. While New Growth Areas are the easiest to develop with transit and pedestrian-oriented patterns, there is a caveat: they also may spread the size of the city. In many cases transit service to these sites is only at preliminary planning stages and they may be required to function for some time without full transit service. In these larger areas the concept should be applied in a manner that respects environmental constraints, works with topography, and functions in the interim without strong transit service.

Every piece of land in the USA is controlled by codes and planning documents that evolved after WWII. These controls have been largely founded on modernist principles – segregation of uses, circulation systems focused on the car, and a loss of public orientation for buildings and gathering places. With the exception of a few urban centers, every city, county, and town has a set of zoning ordinances, planning codes, street standards, and perhaps a comprehensive plan that binds the area to a future of sprawl-like development. To redirect the form of growth for the next generation, each of these documents must be revised. The TOD guidelines provide an overview, a set of goals, and a specific set of principles to direct such revisions. Each case and each place will have unique and special conditions which should enhance, modify, and extend the concepts inherent in the guidelines. But underlying the specifics of each place are some universal postulates of human scale, environmental limits, and social order. These postulates define a new template for growth, one formed to the technology, economics, demographics, and culture of our time.

There are four layers of planning that are affected by this change: regional plans, Comprehensive Plans, Specific Area Plans, and zoning ordinances. Regional planning, though rarely implemented in the U.S., should shape the overall distribution of development, coordinate transit and circulation, balance jobs and housing in an economic fashion, administer regional pollution controls, and set limits to protect open space resources. Without such a regional framework, the local jurisdictions often compete with and contradict one another.

Each "layer" of existing plans needs change. The Comprehensive Plans for each city, town, or county should be updated, or in some cases created from scratch. Local ordinances and standards eventually should be rewritten to allow mixed-use and more walkable neighborhoods,

and to eliminate the current bias toward the auto. An additional planning tool should be developed to allow site-specific, integrated planning for areas larger than single parcels but smaller than those typically covered in community plans. This tool would be similar to the Specific Plan used in many areas of California.

These guidelines were distilled from work in several sub-regional areas: the County of Sacramento, Tri-Met in Portland, the Santa Clara Transit Authority, and the City of San Diego. Within these areas the primary focus for the regional elements of the guidelines was the relationship of development to an expanding transit system. In order to complete the picture at a regional scale, the placement of growth should also be directed by an analysis of long-term open space needs, natural resource assets, and the establishment of an Urban Growth Boundary. The Sacramento County General Plan update proposes such a boundary within its jurisdiction and identifies the critical agricultural lands and river zones that should be permanently preserved.

Identifying rational infill and revitalization districts, New Growth Areas and potential New Town sites should be the work of an agency which spans the numerous cities and counties within a metropolitan area. Lacking such entities, counties, air quality boards, and regional transportation agencies often take on the task without legal power to fully implement the results. Regional governments are needed if growth is to be managed and directed in a sustainable manner.

The Comprehensive Plan establishes each jurisdiction's fundamental goals and policies along with its basic distribution of land uses and development controls. This plan is often completed without real regard for regional concerns and sometimes exhibits a parochial or even xenophobic quality. For example, parts of Placer County represent an excellent growth area for the Sacramento Metropolitan Region, but Placer's Comprehensive Plan effectively limits growth in this area by zoning for higher-income households and open space. In another adjacent jurisdiction, West Sacramento, development is welcomed even when the sites would replace prime agriculture. Each jurisdiction is acting according to its perceived local interests, but the regional impact is a poor distribution of development.

At the same time that Comprehensive Plans rarely express regional intelligence, their goals and policies are often too vague to redirect the quality of growth. The land use map of the Comprehensive Plan typically reinforces the segregation of uses into generic single-use types. There is no "mixed-use" or equivalent designation. The typical zoning map further reinforces the isolation of uses while its ordinances require many features which frustrate the goals of a more integrated mixed-use environment. Finally, the street standards adopted by most areas are myopic, favoring the auto over all other concerns and reinforcing the notion that streets must form a hierarchy of speed and capacity rather than a network of parallel routes and walkable places.

Each level of our planning codes needs revision and updating, but the sequence is key to the result. First, broadly based community support for the alternatives to sprawl must be developed. Before any plan revisions begin, a common understanding that there are significant alternatives to sprawl and that they are bound by specific principles must be developed within all segments of the community. The TOD guidelines can be used as a point of reference in this process. Developers, environmentalists, neighborhood groups, bankers, business interests, and politicians should participate in an effort to redefine the quality and form of growth in their region.

A good example of this inclusionary effort was used in developing and adopting the guidelines for San Diego. Such a common vision and consensus is essential to the scale and political complexity of revising the many layers of planning controls and legislation.

With a clarified common vision, the task of creating a regional framework for growth is possible. One special element of the regional plan should be identification of potential transit corridors and sites for TODs. These "corridor plans" often cross jurisdictional lines and need to be coordinated by a regional planning agency along with the regional transportation agency. Regional plans and "corridor plans," along with the goals and policies of the community consensus, could then be used to guide a revision of each local Comprehensive Plan. The Comprehensive Plan ought to support the emerging regional vision and prescribe a new standard of development. Here again, the guidelines can be referenced as policies and standards to clarify what is meant by mixed-use development. For areas identified with major infill or new growth, Specific Plans should be prepared which detail the application of the guidelines. Finally, the zoning ordinances ought to be updated or supplemented with new standards. In some cases, a new ordinance can be created to guide development in TOD areas while only modifying the existing zoning elements.

The Structure of the Guidelines

The TOD guidelines are designed to provide direction and policies for all levels of planning: regional, comprehensive, specific area, and zoning ordinances. They are expected to be modified for each region and locality, and are not intended as a universal model. At each level of planning, sections of the guidelines can play a greater or lesser role. For example, the Definitions and Guiding Principles sections can be used for regional and comprehensive plan direction, while the sections on streets or specific uses can be used for more detailed zoning ordinance modifications. Taken together, they represent a new vision for the kinds of places we build, and amount to a detailed statement of progressive community goals and the means to achieve those goals.

The guidelines are arranged from the general to the specific. The Definitions and Guiding Principles sections form a summary of concepts. These two sections can stand alone. The Ecology and Habitat section defines in a general sense goals and techniques to make growth more environmentally sensitive and site-specific. The next four sections – on commercial, residential, secondary areas, and parks and civic uses – focus on the nature and quality of each of the primary elements of a TOD. Finally, the remaining sections deal with differing aspects of the circulation system, streets, pedestrian and bicycle environments, transit stops, and parking. The following is a summary of each section with a focus on the critical changes each calls for.

DEFINITIONS   The fundamental building blocks of the guidelines are three "new" land use types: Urban TODs, Neighborhood TODs, and Secondary Areas. These new land use types differ from one another in their varying mix of uses, their relationship to transit, and their density. They differ from most existing zone classifications because they have defined spatial limits relating to the pedestrian scale, and they are mixed-use. The mix of uses – commercial, residential, and public – are defined with minimum densities and land areas, rather than the maximum limits typically found in old zoning codes. Finally, three locations are identified in which TODs can occur: Redevelopable, Infill, and New Growth Sites.

GUIDING PRINCIPLES   The basic principles for all TODs, regardless of type or location, are simple: they must be mixed-use, transit-oriented, walkable, and diverse. Reordering private space to make the public domain more usable, memorable, and the focus of each neighborhood is an overarching goal. The principles may seem radical and familiar at the same time. Making such changes would reverse forty years of planning that put cars ahead of pedestrians, put private space before public, put segregation and isolation of uses before integrated and diversity. To accomplish these types of integration, we should look beyond individual parcels and develop a process that allows larger areas to be planned in a coordinated way.

ECOLOGY AND HABITAT   The Next American Metropolis needs a broad array of environmental strategies at all scales: Urban Growth Boundaries, greenbelts, biological sewage treatment systems, water reclamation, drainage systems that maintain natural water flows, indigenous and drought-tolerant landscaping, and energy conservation techniques in buildings. They are approaches too long ignored in an era of cheap energy, free water, and relative environmental neglect.

CORE COMMERCIAL AREAS   This section outlines some significant evolutions for retail development, both in terms of location and configuration. Creating accessible commercial centers from both local and arterial streets, placing an emphasis on the needs of pedestrians, and integrating retail with civic and transit uses would represent a considerable change from the current norm. These are clearly the most challenging transformations called for by the guidelines and ones that will take time, experimentation, and evolution. Hybrids between our old "Main Street" configurations and our newer strip and mall configurations will be neccessary to combine the needs of walkable neighborhoods with large-scale convenience retail. Additionally, retail development will typically be last to develop in new neighborhoods – which raises questions about phasing and interim development patterns.

RESIDENTIAL AREAS   The key to the housing program for TODs is diversity and flexibility. By defining an average minimum density, the guidelines allow considerable flexibility for developers to invent new combinations of housing types. The guidelines outline several new types of housing to fill the gap between conventional single-family and multi-family needs, including courtyard cottages, small-lot single-family, and ancillary units. These higher-density forms could provide affordable alternatives while maintaining the ownership patterns and private yard features of the single-family home. With these new types of housing mixed with traditional attached housing, the makeup of a TOD residential area can respond to many dimensions of the housing market. This idea of mixing a broad range of housing types is timely because many land developers are coming to understand the wisdom of market diversity. Nevertheless, the challenge of mixing housing types and economies is difficult in an industry and market accustomed to isolated enclaves.

SECONDARY AREAS   These lower-density areas within a mile of transit represent a desirable place for the housing and low-intensity employment uses typical of the modern suburb. The quantity of land allocated for this use will establish the fundamental single-family/multi-family housing ratio for a region. The difference between a Secondary Area and a conventional subdivision is found in its street pattern. The Secondary Area is close enough for walking and biking, and is directly linked by local streets to the mixed-use TOD. Its streets are tree-lined and comfortable to walk along. It is an area which integrates schools, neighborhood parks, and some employment into an accessible framework.

PARKS, PLAZAS, AND CIVIC BUILDINGS   Over the last generation parks have grown larger and more remote. The small neighborhood park and village green have been eliminated in favor of larger facilities (and their reduced maintenance costs) or useless "buffer zones." These guidelines call for a return to local, accessible parks. They also call for prominent locations for civic and public buildings to add identity and focus to the neighborhood. This highlighting of civic facilities along with the requirement to combine them with commercial development represents another new direction. The careful placement of elementary schools at the periphery of TODs is critical because one of the most common pedestrian trips is to school.

STREETS AND CIRCULATION SYSTEM   Traffic is one of the most important and controversial aspects of TODs. Reducing street widths to slow traffic and make pedestrian crossings comfortable is difficult. Although empirical studies have shown that narrow streets are safer, changing the current standards raises issues of legal liability. Even though simple feasibility demonstrations show that fire trucks, school buses, and other large vehicles can safely use such streets, care must be taken in detailing intersections and landscaping. The other significant change outlined is the elimination of simplistic street hierarchies – "connector" streets rather than "collector" streets are needed. High design speeds, responsible for our familiar sweeping turns and large lane widths, should be reduced within the TOD. There is no reason to design for 35–45 mph in a mixed-use pedestrian zone.

PEDESTRIAN AND BICYCLE SYSTEM   The purpose of these guidelines is to encourage streets that are comfortable, interesting and safe to walk along rather than segregated pathways which isolate the pedestrian and result in an expensive, duplicative system. This is the reverse of the popular "Radburn" system of pedestrian "greenways" in that it uses the street as the common ground of the neighborhood. Similarly, the emphasis for bikes should be to integrate them on the street rather than create a separate network. Within TODs it is better to slow cars down to allow bikers safety and comfort on the local streets. However, a larger bike trail system connecting TODs with regional destinations can benefit from separated rights-of-way. Streets should be seen as a multi-purpose mixing ground rather than a single-use utility for cars.

TRANSIT SYSTEM Land use and transit systems must be planned together. This may seem obvious, but for too long the two have been disconnected. Unfortunately, transit systems have been overlaid on inappropriate densities or uses and station areas have been designed as bus transfer zones or park-and-ride lots. Often, trunk line systems follow existing growth in suburban areas rather than helping to define needed New Growth Areas which, in turn, can be planned in a transit-oriented fashion. Transit systems should help guide regional growth and land use, and transit stations should be treated as neighborhood and community focal points. Placing stations at the center of mixed-use commercial and residential neighborhoods will increase ridership as it allows people to combine errands on foot. Trunk line systems should be designed to allow "walk-and-ride" or "bike-and-ride" rather than "park-and-ride" as the central means of access.

PARKING REQUIREMENTS AND CONFIGURATION The handmaids of streets designed for the speed and comfort of cars are large parking lots. The size, location, and configuration of parking lots send a clear and simple message: "arrive by car only." In mixed-use areas several strategies should be employed to reduce the functional and aesthetic dominance of parking lots. On-street parking should be credited, the number of stalls should be reduced to reflect the joint-use time of day or time of week needs of different uses, and lower standards should be set to reflect non-auto arrival modes – transit, bike, or pedestrian. Where possible, parking lots should be placed to the rear of buildings with entries and windows fronting on streets and sidewalks. Reducing and relocating parking lots will be a difficult change, as developers do not want to be at a disadvantage in competing with conventional projects. This is why city- or region-wide standards should be established.

Definitions

Transit-Oriented Development (TOD)

A Transit-Oriented Development (TOD) is a mixed-use community within an average 2,000-foot walking distance of a transit stop and core commercial area. TODs mix residential, retail, office, open space, and public uses in a walkable environment, making it convenient for residents and employees to travel by transit, bicycle, foot, or car.

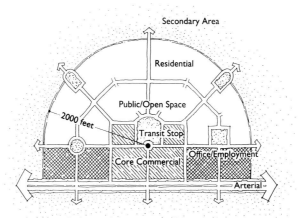

TODs offer an alternative to traditional development patterns by providing housing, services, and employment opportunities for a diverse population in a configuration that facilitates pedestrian and transit access.

They can be developed throughout a metropolitan region on undeveloped sites in urbanizing areas, sites with the potential for redevelopment or reuse, and in new urban growth areas. Their uses and configuration must relate to existing surrounding neighborhoods.

They must be located on or near existing or planned segments of a trunk transit line or feeder bus network. Adequate auto accessibility is also important. These design guidelines establish standards for site selection and development to ensure that TODs succeed in providing a mix of uses, a variety of housing types, and a physical environment that is conducive to pedestrian and transit travel. Developing a network of TODs throughout the region will also serve to strengthen the overall performance of the regional transit system.

The size of a TOD must be determined on a case-by-case basis. The average 2,000-foot radius is intended to represent a "comfortable walking distance" (±10 minutes) for a majority of people. In some locations, comfortable walking distance is affected by topography, climate, intervening arterials or freeways, and other physical features. Therefore, their size will be greater or lesser depending on surrounding features.

Urban TOD

Urban TODs are located directly on the trunk line transit network: at light rail, heavy rail, or express bus stops. They should be developed with high commercial intensities, job clusters, and moderate to high residential densities.

Each TOD may assume a different character and mix of uses depending on its location within the region, market demands, and the surrounding land uses. Urban TODs are suitable for job-generating and high-intensity uses such as offices, community-serving retail centers, and moderate- to high-density housing because they allow direct access to the transit system without requiring passengers to transfer. Similarly, the intensity of development along the trunk line network should reflect the significant investment necessary to construct the transit system and should generate the greatest number of transit-bound trips.

Special development guidelines are recommended for sites that are highly accessible by trunk line transit to permit higher-density residential development and to encourage a higher percentage of job-generating uses. When Urban TODs are located in existing developed neighborhoods, it may be appropriate to apply the densities and mix of uses recommended by a local planning effort. Urban TODs are typically sited approximately 1/2 to 1 mile apart to meet station spacing guidelines, although they could be sited closer together, as transit planning and market demand permit.

Neighborhood TOD

Neighborhood TODs are located on a local or feeder bus line within 10 minutes transit travel time (no more than 3 miles) from a trunk line transit stop. They should place an emphasis on moderate density residential, service, retail, entertainment, civic, and recreational uses.

Neighborhood TODs should have a residential and local-serving shopping focus at densities appropriate for its context and lesser transit service level. Where the feeder bus stops are frequent, TODs can be sited close together and form a "corridor" of moderate density, mixed-use nodes.

Neighborhood TODs can help provide affordable communities because they include a variety of housing types to meet the needs of our increasingly diverse population in a land use pattern that minimizes the need for multiple car ownership. If properly designed, Neighborhood TODs can meet local needs for public facilities and parks, respect the character and quality of existing neighborhoods, and limit inter-community traffic through residential areas. They are also walkable communities, providing access for children, the elderly, and those adults who choose to walk or bike.

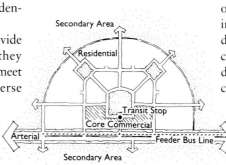

Core Commercial Areas

Each TOD must have a mixed-use core commercial area located adjacent to the transit stop. At a minimum, the core area should provide convenience retail and local-serving offices. Larger core areas may also combine major supermarkets, restaurants, service commercial, entertainment uses, comparison retail, second-floor residential, and employment-intensive office and light industrial uses.

A commercial core at the center of each TOD is essential because it permits most residents and employees to walk or ride bicycles for many basic goods and services. This is particularly advantageous for those without cars and individuals with mobility limitations. Those who still choose to drive to shop will have to go fewer miles and can avoid using arterial streets for local trips. Core commercial areas also provide a mixed-use destination that makes transit use attractive. People are more prone to use transit to get to work if the transit stop is combined with retail and service opportunities.

The size and location of core commercial areas should reflect anticipated market demand, proximity to transit and phasing considerations. Optional upper-floor office and residential uses in the core commercial area increase the mixed-use, round-the-clock nature of the core area. Employment-generating uses, such as office buildings and employee-intensive light industrial uses, may be located adjacent to or amongst the retail component of the core commercial area. The transit stop and core commercial area should be complemented with a "village green" or public plaza which can serve as a focal point for community activities. Secure and convenient bicycle parking facilities should be provided to encourage bicycle access.

Residential Areas

TOD residential areas include housing that is within a convenient walking distance from core commercial areas and transit stops. Residential density requirements should be met with a mix of housing types, including small lot single-family, townhomes, condominiums, and apartments.

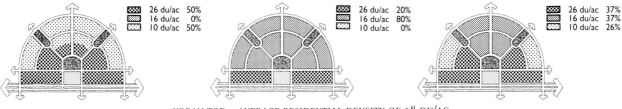

	26 du/ac	50%
	16 du/ac	0%
	10 du/ac	50%

	26 du/ac	20%
	16 du/ac	80%
	10 du/ac	0%

	26 du/ac	37%
	16 du/ac	37%
	10 du/ac	26%

URBAN TOD – AVERAGE RESIDENTIAL DENSITY OF 18 DU/AC

TOD residential areas provide a higher concentration of households in close proximity to transit service and core commercial areas than typical suburban land use patterns.

Average minimum densities of at least 10 du/net acre are necessary to support local bus service; higher densities are necessary for adequate light rail and express bus service. To this end, the TOD concept encourages walking and biking, reduces reliance on the automobile, supports transit service, and creates distinct, identifiable neighborhoods.

Residential areas should extend from the core commercial area and transit stop over an area that is an average 2,000 feet in radius, representing a 10-minute walking distance. They should contain a variety of housing types and ownership patterns, ranging from small-lot single-family homes with carriage units to apartment buildings.

The average minimum density requirement is intended to set a baseline density standard for all TODs, as well as encourage variety. A mix of housing types may be used within this area, some high density and some low density, provided the overall average minimum density is met. For example, a TOD residential area may include a mix of small lot single-family homes with ancillary units (12 du/acre), townhouses (15 du/acre) and apartments (25 du/acre) combined to meet an average density requirement of 18 du/acre. Net densities are roughly 20% higher than gross densities, once streets and other infrastructure improvements are accounted for. Higher average density standards may be adopted by site-specific plans to respond to locational differences within a community. Community Plans, Specific Plans and/or zoning studies will clarify how the minimum average density standards are applied to individual sites.

Public Uses

Public uses are required to serve residents and workers in TODs and neighboring areas. Parks, plazas, greens, public buildings, and public services may be used to fulfill this requirement. Small public parks and plazas must be provided to meet local population needs.

The structure of a TOD is built around accessible and convenient public facilities and spaces. A strong sense of community, participation, identity, and conviviality is important to support a sense of safety and comfort within a neighborhood. Public uses serve this role by providing meeting places, recreation opportunities and lunch time picnic spots essential to the vitality of TODs. A well-used park is centrally located in a neighborhood, has good visibility from the street, and often benefits by being next to a public library, civic services, transit, or retail.

Each TOD must contain open space areas available to the public and facilities which serve the needs of the surrounding community. Varying sizes and types of TODs will require or justify inclusion of civic buildings and public facilities. Appropriate public facilities include day care, libraries, community buildings, police and fire stations, post offices, and governmental services. Public buildings should be placed in central locations, as highly visible focal points, or adjacent to public parks and plazas. Civic uses such as an urban plaza, community center, post office, and library are best located in the core area in conjunction with retail businesses and offices. Recreation-oriented uses, such as parks, recreation facilities, and community buildings, as well as large parks and schools, should be centrally located with easy access from TOD residences and the core area. Schools should be placed at the perimeter of TODs in their Secondary Area.

Secondary Areas

Each TOD may have a Secondary Area adjacent to it, including areas across an arterial, which are no further than one mile from the core commercial area. The Secondary Area street network must provide multiple direct street and bicycle connections to the transit stop and core commercial area, with a minimum of arterial crossings. Secondary Areas may have lower density single-family housing, public schools, large community parks, low intensity employment-generating uses, and park-and-ride lots.

The Secondary Area provides for uses which are not appropriate in TODs because they are lower density and more auto-oriented. These areas will, however, provide market support for TOD businesses because Secondary Area residents and workers may shop in the core commercial area and generate riders for the transit system. Employment-generating uses should be located directly across the arterial from the transit stop.

Commercial uses which are very similar in nature and market appeal to those located in the core commercial area should not be permitted in Secondary Areas. They may diminish the ability of the TOD to establish a viable retail center. Similarly, very low intensity industrial and warehousing uses which are highly auto- and truck-dependent are not appropriate for Secondary Areas; they do not have a sufficient number of

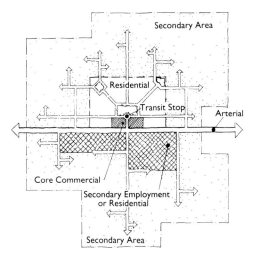

employees to contribute to create a healthy pedestrian environment.

Single-family residential development is and will continue to be an important land use. These areas typically have too low a density to be adequately serviced by transit. By maximizing street connections to TODs and making it convenient for residents to bike or walk to the transit stop, transit utilization in single-family areas may increase. This is important both in New Growth Areas and in existing neighborhoods where streets may need to be retrofitted. Providing multiple, interior street connections between TODs and Secondary Areas will keep many auto trips off arterials. Locating public schools in Secondary Areas will provide a service for the TOD without using valuable transit-accessible land.

Other Uses

Uses that rely extensively upon autos, trucks or have very low employment intensities are not appropriate uses for TODs or Secondary Areas. Rural residential, industrial uses, and travel-commercial complexes should be located outside of TODs and Secondary Areas.

Many uses typically allowed in commercial areas rely predominantly upon auto travel to generate business patrons. These uses, such as auto dealers, freestanding car washes, mini-storage facilities, highway commercial uses, and motels, should not be permitted in TODs or Secondary Areas.

Similarly, low-employment-generating industrial uses should not be permitted in TODs or Secondary Areas.

They are not compatible with nearby residential uses and generate few employees to support core commercial areas. Industrial uses are more appropriate where existing industrial activities occur and where major freeway noise impacts are anticipated.

In order for more frequent transit service to be economically viable, uses near transit stops must have moderate residential densities and the commercial uses must create a high level of pedestrian activity. Land near the transit stop should reinforce transit use by supporting higher density, pedestrian-oriented uses and development patterns. Uses that are primarily auto-oriented are not appropriate for TODs and are better located near major highways.

Location Types

TODs may be located in Redevelopable Sites, Infill Sites, or in New Growth Areas. Redevelopable Sites are developed areas that could be revitalized with new, more intensive uses and transit service. Infill Sites are vacant parcels surrounded by existing urban development. New Growth Areas are larger, undeveloped properties typically on the city's periphery. Regional comprehensive plans, local community plans, and transit corridor plans should identify appropriate sites in each of these settings.

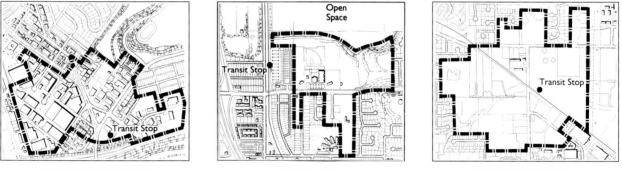

REDEVELOPABLE SITE   INFILL SITE   NEW GROWTH AREA

TODs are an opportunity to promote efficient development patterns, both in the existing urbanized fabric of the city and in New Growth Areas. Three types of settings have been identified which broadly characterize the physical pattern of development throughout most American cities. These three functional settings represent the range of conditions where TODs could be located and linked by transit.

Implementation on Redevelopable and Infill Sites has the opportunity to transform development patterns that are presently highly auto-oriented into mixed-use, transit-oriented development. Careful site selection and integration of viable, existing uses within the site and its surroundings can help ensure its future success.

Furthermore, traffic and infrastructure constraints must be addressed if TODs are to function well.

The TOD concept is also a strategy to promote efficient and environmentally sensitive development patterns in newly developing areas. Because these sites are relatively free of existing land uses, New Growth Areas offer a great opportunity for creating mixed-use destinations and interconnected street systems. Constraints generated from topography and sensitive habitats can be overcome by carefully selecting sites and by configuring streets to relate to the topography. A fundamental premise, however, must be to limit sprawl by clustering development within planned urban growth areas.

Guiding Principles

Relationship to Transit and Circulation

The site must be located on an existing or planned trunk transit line or on a feeder bus route within 10 minutes transit travel time from a stop on the trunk line. Where transit may not occur for a period of time, the land use and street patterns within a TOD must function effectively in the interim.

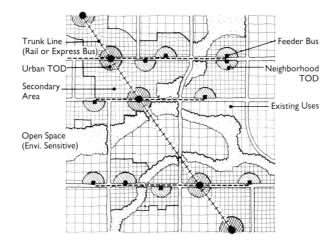

The trunk line network represents the region's express transit system. It typically consists of either light rail, heavy rail, or express bus service, with at least a 15-minute frequency of service and a dedicated right-of-way. Providing a dedicated right-of-way, whether fixed rail or HOV lanes, serves two important purposes: 1) it ensures expedited and free-flow transit travel; and 2) it represents a long-term transit commitment that allows developers to make similar investments.

The feeder bus network is a system of timed transfer local bus routes that link to the trunk line network. Transit stops on the feeder bus network should be within 10 minutes transit travel time (approximately 2 to 3 miles) from a trunk line network stop, with buses running at least a 15-minute frequency of service. 10 minutes transit travel time is the maximum people are typically willing to ride prior to a mode change. In some circumstances, a feeder bus can be provided by a private transit system that meets this level of service criteria.

Even with an ambitious 40% non-auto mode split, 60% of all trips will continue to be via autos. The land use patterns in TODs, as well as their internal street systems, must plan for on-going auto use. Adequate auto access from arterials and freeways, as well as frequent transit service, will also be an important locational consideration for the more intensive, employment-oriented TODs. Not all transit stops will be TODs; some stops will be developed as park-and-ride lots.

In many locations transit service is planned, but will not be implemented until well after development ocurrs. A region has the opportunity to guide transit planning by providing the densities necessary to support transit with advanced land use planning. In early years, express bus service can serve planned light rail lines and establish ridership clientele. Land use patterns should lead transit service planning, rather than expecting transit to come to an area that must be retrofitted to provide transit-supportable densities.

Mix of Uses

All TODs must be mixed-use and contain a minimum amount of public, core commercial and residential uses. Vertical mixed-use buildings are encouraged, but are considered a bonus to the basic horizontal mixed-use requirement. The following is a preferred mix of land uses, by percent of land area within a TOD:

USE	NEIGHBORHOOD TOD	URBAN TOD
Public	10% - 15%	5% - 15%
Core/Employment	10% - 40%	30% - 70%
Housing	50% - 80%	20% - 60%

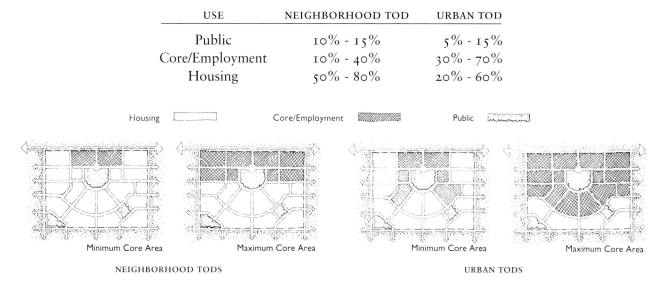

Housing   Core/Employment   Public

Minimum Core Area	Maximum Core Area		Minimum Core Area	Maximum Core Area
NEIGHBORHOOD TODS			URBAN TODS	

A certain minimum proportion of uses is required to stimulate pedestrian activity and to provide economic incentives for developing with mixed-use patterns. The proportion of uses is based on site area, not density or building intensity. It does not preclude additional, different uses on upper floors. At a minimum, retail, housing, and public uses are required in all TODs. Employment uses within the core commercial area may be used to augment these minimum uses, as market conditions permit. The public use component should include land devoted to parks, plazas, open space, and public facilities. The different mix of uses for Neighborhood TODs and Urban TODs is intended to reflect the variations in intensity and type of development desired at these sites.

The mix of land uses and appropriate densities should be clarified in a community or site-specific planning process, in order to address site-related issues such as context, market demand, topography, infrastructure capacity, transit service frequency, and arterial/freeway accessibility. Special care should be taken to respect the context of the site and the character of surrounding existing neighborhoods.

Vertical mixed-use buildings do contribute to a healthy pedestrian environment, but are much more difficult to implement due to current real estate practices that encourage single-use buildings. For this reason, vertical mixed-use should not be solely relied upon to create pedestrian-oriented places.

If a neighborhood or employment area has local destinations within convenient walking distance, residents and employees are more likely to walk or bicycle. Furthermore, if local destinations are accessible to drivers without requiring use of the arterial street system, congestion can be reduced. The required proportion of uses is designed to encourage pedestrian activity, yet allow flexibility to create neighborhoods with different use emphases, such as primarily residential TODs (Neighborhood TODs) and TODs which emphasize job-generating uses (Urban TODs).

Residential Mix

A mix of housing densities, ownership patterns, price, and building types is desirable in a TOD. Average minimum densities should vary between 10 and 25 dwelling units/net residential acre, depending on the relationship to surrounding existing neighborhoods and location within the urban area.

Small-Lot Single-Family

Townhouses

Duplexes

Apartments & Condominiums

While each TOD will take on a different character and will have a different proportion of single-family and multi-family densities, care should be taken to provide a variety of housing types, costs, and ownership opportunities. Residential areas can combine small lot single-family units, duplexes, townhouses, and apartment buildings.

In order for TODs to be affordable to the diverse range of households, they must provide a mix of housing types. Single-family housing has, and will continue to have, strong market demand in most communities. Higher density townhouses and multi-family units are, however, gaining an increasing proportion of the market share. The range of permissible residential densities can accommodate all of these household needs. Providing a mix of housing types will also result in more "cosmopolitan" communities.

Street and Circulation System

The local street system should be recognizable, formalized, and inter-connected, converging to transit stops, core commercial areas, schools and parks. Multiple and parallel routes must be provided between the core commercial area, residential, and employment uses so that local trips are not forced onto arterial streets. Streets must be pedestrian friendly; sidewalks, street trees, building entries, and parallel parking must shelter and enhance the walking environment.

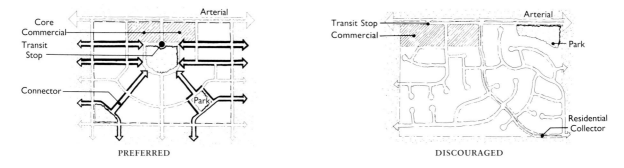

PREFERRED

DISCOURAGED

The street pattern should be simple, memorable, and direct, avoiding circuitous routes. Streets should converge at common destinations, such as transit stops, core commercial areas, and parks. They should allow autos, bikes, and pedestrians to travel on small local streets to any location in the TOD without crossing or following an arterial. Street connections should be designed to keep through trips on arterial streets and local trips within neighborhoods. At no time should an arterial street be the only route to and from the different land uses of the TOD.

Where there is steep topography or other sensitive natural resources, it may be necessary to curve streets and create some cul-de-sacs. On-street pedestrian and bicycle paths should be provided to allow residents to walk to all local destinations, rather than segregated off-street paths.

Clear, formalized, and inter-connected street systems make common destinations visible. They also provide the shortest and most direct path for pedestrians and bicyclists. With an inter-connected street system, any single street will be less likely to be overburdened by excessive traffic, thus reducing the need for cul-de-sacs. A street pattern which is circuitous and complex will discourage pedestrians; a street system with landmarks and a simple form will be memorable and familiar.

General Design Criteria

Buildings should address the street and sidewalk with entries, balconies, porches, architectural features, and activities which help create safe, pleasant walking environments. Building intensities, orientation, and massing should promote more active commercial centers, support transit, and reinforce public spaces. Variation and human-scale detail in architecture is encouraged. Parking should be placed to the rear of buildings.

Orienting buildings to public streets will encourage walking by providing easy pedestrian connections, by bringing activities and visually interesting features closer to the street, and by providing safety through watchful eyes. Moderate-to-high intensities and densities also support frequent and convenient transit service. Retail centers with pedestrian-scale features and configurations will support the walking environment critical to that transit service.

With the possible exception of anchor retail stores, primary building entrances should be physically and visually oriented toward streets, parks and plazas, and not to the interior of blocks or to parking lots and garages. Parking lots should be placed to the rear of buildings. Secondary entrances, oriented toward parking lots, are permitted. Where existing viable uses are separated from the street by large parking lots, infill is encouraged at the street. In addition, new internal streets may be constructed closer to existing entries, thus creating a "Main Street" pedestrian setting.

Core commercial areas should be intensive enough to provide a "Main Street" shopping spine. Furthermore, multi-storied buildings and structured parking are strongly encouraged in Urban TODs to better utilize land adjacent to a transit line. As a region continues to grow, land economics may make future intensification desirable. Commercial area development plans should include long-term strategies for additional stories and buildings, along with structured parking. Residential infill should also be possible by permitting some ancillary dwellings in single-family residential areas.

Site Boundary Definition

The size of the TOD is variable depending on the ability to provide internal, local street connections. Parcels within an average 10-minute walking distance of the transit stop shall be included if direct access by local street or path can be established without use of an arterial. To allow for a basic mix of uses, the TOD area should be a minimum of 10 acres for Redevelopable and Infill Sites, and 40 acres for New Growth Areas.

While the majority of the site should be within a quarter to half mile walking distance, the total area will vary based on parcel sizes, topography and other intervening features. Oddly shaped parcels may extend the site boundary beyond 2,000 feet to include areas which are the equivalent of a 10 minute walking distance; sites limited by topography or adjacent to freeways or arterials may be smaller. Where a majority of a parcel is within 2,000 feet, the whole parcel should be included in the site area. The distance from the transit stop to the outer boundary of the Secondary Area should be no greater than one mile. The arterial network in a New Growth Area should be located to maximize the potential size of TODs and not bisect viable sites.

If a candidate site does not have a street system that can provide direct auto and walking connections to the core area and transit stop, the site must be strictly limited to the parcels that do or can provide connections. This site may be a single property, but must be a mini-

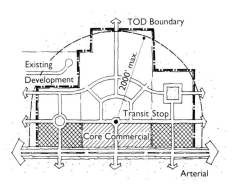

mum of 10 acres in size. All required uses must be provided within this smaller site area.

Sufficient vacant or redevelopable land must be available in the site to allow full application of the development standards. In Redevelopable Areas, there should be a mix of underutilized properties that could be redeveloped to more intensive uses. On Infill Sites, the undeveloped parcel should be surrounded by uses that fit with the TOD concept. Adjacent existing uses, such as employment or multi-family housing, can essentially function as part of the TOD or its Secondary Area if their intensities and densities are consistent with the design guidelines.

Sites in New Growth Areas may consist of 40 to 160 acres of land that are wholly undeveloped or have some minor amount of existing uses. Sites may consist of parcels in multiple ownerships provided that the planning for the designated site is coordinated among the property owners.

Coordinated Planning and Specific Area Plans

Regardless of the number of property owners, development of a TOD must provide a coordinated plan for the entire site. This "Specific Area Plan" should be consistent with the Design Guidelines, coordinate development across property lines, and provide strategies for financing construction of public improvements.

TODs represent a departure from traditional single parcel/single use development and require coordinated planning and implementation of public improvements such as streets, pedestrian paths, bikeways, and plazas. While a few sites will be owned by a single entity, many sites will consist of numerous parcels under multiple ownerships. To ensure that the area is planned in a coordinated manner, a single plan should be developed. Property owners may jointly prepare a single development plan or work cooperatively with the local jurisdiction to prepare a Specific Plan.

There are several aspects of a Specific Plan that can expedite and reduce costs in the development process. Specific Plans allow street alignments and land use configurations to be planned across property lines in order to achieve community goals that are broader than a single parcel; standard zoning and PUDs cannot ensure this level of coordination. A common Environmental Impact Report may be prepared for the entire Specific Plan area, freeing individual property owners from duplicative analyses and lengthy and expensive review processes. Specific design guidelines and development standards for the site can be prepared which replace restrictive and inappropriate elements of the local zoning ordinances, as well as encourage design qualities appropriate in mixed-use areas.

Implementation plans should be prepared as part of every Specific Plan. These plans should include financing strategies to ensure that public improvements, such as schools, parks, public facilities, roads, and other infrastructure are build in a coordinated and timely manner, and that the cost of those improvements is equitably distributed among property owners and other beneficiaries.

Distribution of TODs

TODs should be located to maximize access to their Core Commercial Areas from surrounding areas without relying solely on arterials. TODs with major competing retail centers should be spaced a minimum of one mile apart and should be distributed to serve different neighborhoods. When located on fixed rail transit systems, they should be located to allow efficient station spacing.

Appropriate TOD spacing provides convenience retail opportunities that are within an easy walk for most residents, ensures the viability of the retail centers, and better links transit stops to concentrations of residents and core commercial services.

TODs should be distributed throughout a New Growth Area in a pattern that allows the greatest number of residents and workers access to a variety of shopping opportunities. They should also be

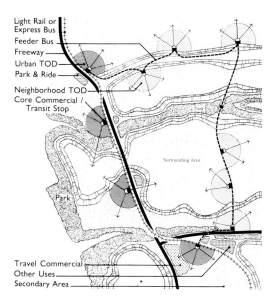

Light Rail or Express Bus
Feeder Bus
Freeway
Urban TOD
Park & Ride
Neighborhood TOD
Core Commercial / Transit Stop
Park
Travel Commercial
Other Uses
Secondary Area
Park
Surrounding Area

distributed to permit residents to walk to retail and public facilities without having to cross an arterial street, whenever possible. The one-mile spacing guideline relates to the market area necessary to support a grocery store (often the anchor store in a neighborhood shopping center), as well as being a typical spacing for transit stops. Shopping centers with uses that are not directly competing may be sited closer than one mile apart.

Redevelopable and Infill Sites

Redevelopable and Infill Sites should develop underutilized parcels with new uses that allow them to function as walkable, mixed-use districts. Existing uses which are complementary, economical, and physically viable should be integrated into the form and function of the neighborhood. Existing low-intensity and auto-oriented uses should be redeveloped to be consistent with the TOD's compact, pedestrian-oriented character.

BEFORE

AFTER

BEFORE

AFTER

As land values increase over time or as the result of transit investments, older neighborhoods may gradually transition to new uses and economically underutilized areas may redevelop to more intensive uses. TODs may be able to take advantage of this change to reinforce the transit system with pedestrian-oriented land uses. Existing on-site uses that are economically viable can serve as the starting point and in some cases will represent the nucleus for future economic revitalization. The condition, density, and intensity of these existing uses must be compatible or be made compatible with pedestrian and transit travel. New uses which are missing from the ideal mix of land uses can be introduced. Uses which rely solely on auto trips, such as gas stations, car washes, storage facilities, motels, or low-intensity industrial uses, are not likely to contribute to pedestrian activity in the TOD and should be discouraged. Intensification and redevelopment must, however, be balanced with sensitivity to protecting existing neighborhoods and to the problems of gentrification.

Site plans should integrate existing uses by respecting their on-going operations, basic access requirements, and, if appropriate, existing building massing and architecture. Site improvements may be required to make these properties more pedestrian-oriented. Infill buildings may be needed to meet density and intensity requirements and to better address streets. Safe, direct and pleasant pedestrian connections should be provided to surrounding areas. Site landscaping and building frontage treatments may also be needed to enhance streets and mitigate areas where streetside conditions,

such as parking, blank walls, and service entries, are unavoidable. If these guidelines cannot be met initially, plans for implementing necessary improvements over time should be developed.

Infill Sites represent undeveloped parcels of land that have been "skipped over" in the process of growth and are surrounded by existing development. This can occur in inner-city locations or in suburban areas. In many cases these parcels do not have an established street system, but are connected to surrounding neighborhoods or adjacent to existing commercial developments. These sites are often large enough to develop all or a major portion of a TOD; the existing surrounding neighborhoods will then function as its Secondary Area.

New Growth Areas

New Growth Areas are typically located at the edge of the metropolitan region or on large sites which have been passed over. They may be large enough to create a network of Urban and Neighborhood TODs, as well as Secondary Areas, and should be planned in coordination with extensions of transit and an Urban Growth Boundary. New Growth Areas should not, however, be used to justify "leap frog" development or degrade sensitive environmental habitat or valuable agriculture lands.

BEFORE

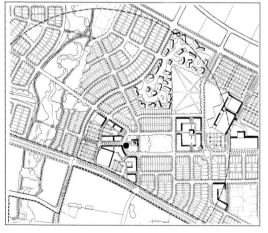

AFTER

A high growth region may need to designate areas at its perimeter to handle the growth not feasibly accommodated in redevelopable or infill locations. New Growth Areas are generally free of existing urban uses and are therefore often the easiest to develop with transit- and pedestrian-oriented land use patterns. However, because they are generally located at the edge of urban development, they may ultimately spread the size of the city.

A key criterion for selecting New Growth Areas should be transit system viability once the area is fully built-out. Areas that are too distant from the metropolitan center or present expensive obstacles to transit should not be designated for new growth. Corridor plans should be prepared along planned transit lines to select appropriate sites for tods and determine whether sufficient ridership can be generated along the entire corridor.

Development within New Growth Areas should be located along existing or planned trunk transit lines, and developed as tods and associated Secondary Areas. This is part of a strategy to maximize preservation of open space, focus development potential into pedestrian-oriented patterns that can be served by transit, and limit urban sprawl. While some sites may only have sufficient land to develop a single Urban or Neighborhood tod, many sites are large enough to create a network of tods, each served by transit, thus stimulating a significant positive impact in local travel behavior and congestion trends. Site-specific plans should be prepared to ensure that environmental constraints are respected.

Because it may be a number of years before transit reaches some potential sites, projects should be planned to function in the interim without strong transit service. In initial years, trunk line service may be provided in the form of express buses, with later conversion to light rail. Rights-of-way should be reserved for light rail, exclusive bus lanes, bus turn-outs, and transit stop facilities in the early phases of planning and development.

Regional Form

Regional form should be the product of transit accessibility and environmental constraints. Major natural resources, such as rivers, bays, ridgelands, agriculture, and sensitive habitat should be preserved and enhanced. An Urban Growth Boundary should be established that provides adequate area for growth while honoring these criteria.

Regional growth has been largely directed by highway capacity and location. The cycle starts with housing pioneering more remote sectors of the metropolitan region in the form of bedroom communities. With the federal and state highway investments of the last thirty years, these seemingly remote suburbs and small towns became commute-accessible to the existing major job centers. The remote suburbs offered low-cost land and affordable housing

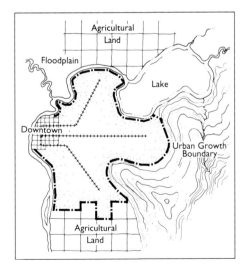

ownership, and therefore viable housing for the regional workforce. Retail, services, recreation, and civic uses followed in proportion to the demand created by the housing. At a critical mass, the new suburban areas began to attract jobs themselves and "Edge Cities," as Joel Garreau calls them, were formed. As these new decentralized job centers grew, the process began again creating another layer of sprawl extending out from the decentralized job centers. Today, the suburb-to-suburb commute now represents forty percent of total commute trips.

The next generation of regional growth is in crisis. Putting aside the environmental and social implications of repeating this old pattern, the highway funds are no longer present to support the next layer of sprawl. The alternative is a regional form which sets reasonable boundaries and directs growth to infill and transit-accessible locations. Natural features can contribute to a justifiable regional boundary that is reinforced from within by strongly supported internal transit corridors.

Regional form is then directed from within, by transit, and from without, by natural boundaries.

It is important that such planning be done with an eye to the long-range needs and implications of growth, and that the area defined has adequate room for urban expansion as well as infill. Constraints that are too tight can easily lead to increased housing costs, flight of working families, and the resultant exodus of jobs. Infill and New Growth Areas that are diverse in their housing profile and transit-supportive can allow a region to retain a healthy job base by providing housing that is affordable and accessible.

Criteria for New Towns

New Towns should only be planned if a region's growth is too large to be directed into Infill and adjacent New Growth Areas. They should be used to preserve the integrity of and separation between existing towns, as well as plan for a regional balance in jobs and housing. Appropriate sites should have a viable commuter transit connection and are not on environmentally sensitive lands.

In rare cases, a region's growth cannot be reasonably contained within Infill and New Growth Areas. This is most common in areas with distinct small towns which want to preserve their character, but are under growth pressure from a nearby metropolitan center. Rather than simply rejecting growth and indirectly propagating piecemeal development in unincorporated or uncontrolled areas, these regions can choose to plan for a coherent New Town. This strategy can help preserve the identity and separation of existing small towns, without instigating sprawl in more remote sites.

Another circumstance for New Towns is the availability of a major site within transit access of a metropolitan center and within an Urban Growth Boundary. This type of site should be planned as a "satellite"

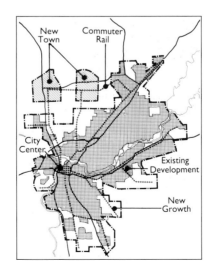

New Town, with a strong jobs/housing balance and a greenbelt separation between existing communities. New Growth Areas and New Towns are similar in this circumstance, but for the size, intensity of jobs, and greenbelt. Such satellite towns can stabilize the edge of a metropolitan region by providing a greenbelt, while absorbing the demand which could fuel sprawl. They also have the advantage in some circumstances of lower land costs and therefore can provide housing at more affordable levels. If planned intelligently, New Towns also can provide infrastructure and services in an efficient form. In contrast, areas in which the existing infrastructure is overburdened and in need of reconstruction and major expansion often have to pay a premium for redevelopment.

Ecology and Habitat

Open Space Resource Protection

Major creeks, riparian habitat, slopes, and other sensitive environmental features should be conserved as open space amenities and incorporated into the design of new neighborhoods. Fencing and piping of creeks should be avoided and channelization should be minimized.

Natural features provide visual relief and establish a unique character for a community. Whenever possible, open space resources should be incorporated into the design of TODs and Secondary Areas. Sensitive site planning should be encouraged so that natural habitats are protected and natural features become an integral part of the community. These resources should be treated as key amenities, rather than as edges to developments.

Natural features can often serve dual purposes, as resource protection and public access. Public access should be permitted while important natural features and sensitive habitats are preserved. Bicycle paths can often be constructed along creek systems, thus serving a dual function of allowing public access to open space and providing paths to destinations along the edges of linear parks. Major public facilities, such as schools, parks, and recreation centers, should be linked by these open space/bicycle trail systems.

Ridgetops and other topographic features should serve as primary urban form determinants. In New Growth Areas, there is an opportunity for open spaces to shape and enhance neighborhoods, to provide a scenic resource from roads, and to serve as permanent wildlife corridors.

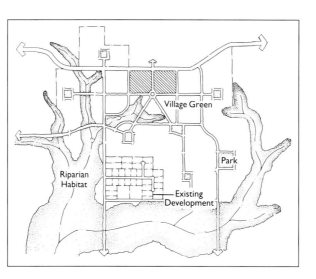

Urban Growth Boundaries

Urban Growth Boundaries (UGB) should be established at the edge of metropolitan regions to protect significant natural resources and provide separation between existing towns and cities. Lands within the UGB should be transit accessible, contiguous to existing development, and planned for long-term urbanization.

Oregon is one of the few states that has enabling legislation for UGBs. Fundamental to such a device are regional governing bodies that have the power to establish and protect limits to growth. The problem of a single jurisdiction establishing such a line is that a simple change of the elected board can reverse or revise the line. A UGB typically has to be created in the context of multiple jurisdictions to be meaningful. One alternative to state-level empowerment or regional governments is a joint power agreement between several jurisdictions. If, for example, a county and several cities were to agree upon a boundary and corresponding holding capacities, any change would require unanimous agreement – an unlikely political event, short of a new regional consensus.

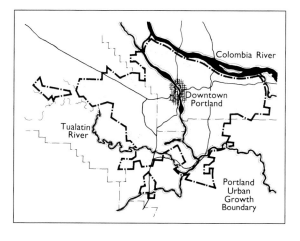

The placement and configuration of a UGB is a complex, site-specific task. It is important that the boundary be large enough to absorb a reasonable amount of growth for a significant period of time. It should not be a mechanism for down-zoning lands imminently vulnerable to development. It is a long-term tool to direct growth and regional form. One of its purposes is to prevent investments from being squandered on land speculation in inappropriate areas. It can serve to keep development intelligent and efforts focused on coherent sites. Such a boundary must respect and protect major environmental assets and integrate the needs of transit. This transit criterion means that there should not be gaps in the urban fabric, and that all areas within the UGB be transit accessible.

Wastewater Treatment and Water Reclamation

On-site wastewater treatment facilities which use biological systems to reclaim water should be used whenever possible. The reclaimed water should be used for on-site irrigation or for nearby farming.

Emerging technologies are allowing more efficient water treatment and re-use at the scale of neighborhoods and small communities. Typically, biological wastewater treatment systems incorporate wetlands, streams and ponds to aerate and dissolve water-borne pollutants. Wastewater is treated to a high level of purification (tertiary treatment), whereas most municipal systems only filter solids (primary treatment) or partially treat the wastewater (secondary treatment). The result is two-fold: recycled water that can either be re-used or filtered back into the

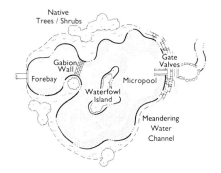

local ecology; and an enhanced on-site riparian system that is an amenity.

Drought conditions and water rationing in many western states are often forcing new development to use this precious resource more responsibly. Water reclamation systems allow a doubling in efficiency by re-using treated wastewater for irrigation. Bio-mass can also be harvested for fertilizer. Farms at the periphery and parks within New Growth Areas can benefit from these new water resources.

Drainage and Wetlands

Existing drainageways and wetlands should be maintained or enhanced in a natural state. In lower-density areas, drainage systems should recharge on-site groundwater by using swales and surface systems, rather than storm drains. All urban runoff must be treated on site with biological retention and filtration areas.

A key element of this approach to community design involves making a stronger connection between nature and our cities. More aggressive approaches should be taken to preserve and repair on-site creeks and riparian habitat, so they can become integral community elements. Many communities, for example, are opening up creeks that have been piped under neighborhoods and business districts, so they can re-emerge as natural local amenities.

New drainage systems in lower-density areas should use shallow open swales and retention ponds that are designed to function effectively during peak flows, create

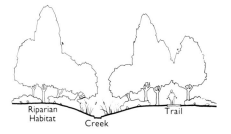

small picnic and play areas during the off-season, and introduce landscape corridors that meander through neighborhoods. This approach is less feasible in high-density areas where land is at a premium. Village Homes, in Davis, CA, for example, uses surface drainageways to collect all storm-water run-off into a creek system that flows throughout this lushly landscaped neighborhood. Small detention areas double as children's play areas; walking paths follow the open space network. Similarly, the lake at Laguna West serves both as a flood detention basin and a biological treatment system for urban run-off.

Indiginous and Drought Tolerant Landscaping

Landscape species used on public and private lands should be indigenous or proven adaptable to the local climate. In areas with water limitations, drought-tolerant species should be used in a majority of sites. Prominent stands of trees should be preserved.

Trees and other landscaping help to establish a distinct character and quality of life for a community. Indigenous species, in particular, create a unique identity and carry forward the history of a place at a scale that is recognizable. Some sites are fortunate to have prominent stands of heritage trees which make identifiable landmarks within the larger community and serve to establish character for newly developing areas. The use of native plants, as well as preservation of existing important natural resources, should be encouraged.

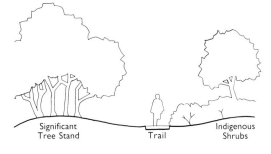

Significant Tree Stand   Trail   Indigenous Shrubs

A number of the elements of mixed-use, higher-density neighborhoods also lead to the need to utilize plant species that are drought-tolerant and adaptable to the local climate. Streets lined with trees, small and frequent parks, and preserved creek corridors all make these compact neighborhoods more livable. In the context of water conservation, use of drought-tolerant species becomes essential. Public areas in particular should serve as models for the private sector in terms of appropriate plant selection and use of landscaping techniques.

Energy Conservation

Energy conservation should be a goal of site, as well as building design. Strategies such as passive solar, natural ventilation, daylighting, and simple shading should be employed when cost effective and appropriate to the climate. Micro-climate effects can be enhanced or mitigated through intelligent building configuration and landscape treatments.

There are several strategies for energy conservation in community planning: reduced auto usage, enhanced microclimate, conservation in buildings, and climate-responsive architecture. Interestingly, they tend to overlap and reinforce one another. For example, an enhanced microclimate, through shade trees or wind barriers, can affect auto usage by creating more comfort for the pedestrian, and simultaneously eliminate the need for architectural shading. Climate-responsive buildings, with courtyards for thermal buffering or clear glass for daylighting, can add interest and safety for the pedestrian and avoid the negative microclimate impacts of

reflected glare or wind tunnel effects. Reduced auto usage can have a positive impact on building energy consumption by reducing asphalt areas and the associated heat buildup. This interaction of effects means that a careful balancing of strategies, appropriate to the climate and region, is important.

In all cases the strategies for buildings should be cost-effective and appropriate to the use and climate. For most mild and partly cloudy climates, insulation and shading are important residential features, while daylighting and natural ventilation are appropriate for commercial buildings. This means that strict solar orientation is not critical in these areas. In cold sunny climates, certain passive solar heating strategies may be cost effective. Here, street and building orientation may be important. It is undesirable in mild climates to attempt passive solar orientation for all buildings, partly because this constrains the site plan too much and partly because passive solar heating in mild climate zones is often less cost effective than super insulation or district heating systems.

Microclimate design strate-

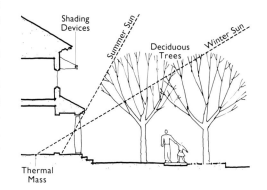

gies provide a wealth of design concepts for community planning. The use of water and landscaping to temper local climate is a well-documented art. In some circumstances building massing and orientation can play a role; narrow streets in hot arid climates and setbacks for solar access in cold climates are two examples. Finally, the building itself can layer the environment with buffer zones of intermediate temperatures: porches, courtyards, overhangs, and trellises are a few such devices.

Core Commercial Areas

Core Commercial Areas Size and Location

The core commercial area may mix ground floor retail, office, and commercial space. It must occupy at least 10 percent of the total TOD site area and have a minimum of 10,000 sq-ft of retail space adjacent to the transit stop.

Mixed-use core commercial areas are the primary link between transit and land use. Sufficient retail and commercial space must be provided to form a useful shopping center and create opportunities for residents and employees to run errands during lunch-time or while traveling to and from work. Without shopping opportunities within convenient walking distance, residents and workers will use their cars for more trips and will lose an incentive to use transit.

While commercial uses do not need to be concentrated in a single location, a minimum amount of retail space should be directly accessible from the transit stop. Appropriate uses include retail shops, professional offices, service commercial uses, restaurants, cinemas, health clubs, and other entertainment facilities. Small hotels, pensioners, and single-room occupancy hotels are also encouraged to provide a greater choice of accommodations near potential transit destinations and to provide needed housing.

The size and mix of uses in each core commercial area can vary depending on the size, location, and overall function of the site in the region. It should, at a minimum, serve as a convenience shopping area for TOD and Secondary Area residents

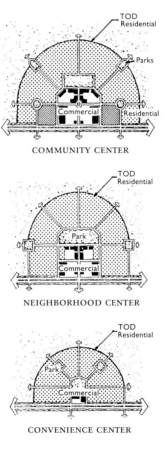

COMMUNITY CENTER

NEIGHBORHOOD CENTER

CONVENIENCE CENTER

and employees. Types of commercial centers include: convenience shopping and services (10,000 to 25,000 sq-ft); neighborhood centers with a supermarket, drugstore, and supporting uses (80,000 to 140,000 sq-ft); specialty retail centers (60,000 to 120,000 sq-ft); and community centers with convenience shopping and department stores (120,000 sq-ft or greater). Other employment-generating uses can be located within the core commercial area to provide a balance to shopping and residential uses.

Street-level retail, office, and service commercial space should form a pedestrian-oriented circulation system that is accessible from the surrounding neighborhood without requiring use of an arterial street. Office and employee-intensive light industrial uses should be located adjacent to the shopping portion of the core commercial area. In redevelopable areas where a connecting street is not possible, at least one pedestrian pathway is required from surrounding areas. Core commercial areas should also be designed to encourage shopping during travel to and from the transit stop or at mid-day by office workers.

Office and Retail Intensities

Intensive office and retail development is strongly encouraged to best utilize land surrounding transit stops. Where feasible, structured parking is encouraged. Offices without structured parking must have a minimum 0.35 Floor Area Ratio (FAR). Retail must have a minimum FAR of 0.30 with surface parking. For both office and retail development, higher than minimum FARS are strongly encouraged; maximums should be set by local plans.

1.00 FAR	0.50 FAR	0.30 FAR

As land values in a region rise, structured parking in selected locations will become economically feasible. This guideline encourages development of multi-story buildings for office and retail uses with structured parking, thereby allowing more efficient use of land in a TOD. Floor Area Ratios represent the proportion of building square footage to land area. For example, an FAR of 1.0 would allow either full coverage of the site with a single-story building, or a two-story building that covers only 50% of the site. Additional setback and build-ing height standards further clarify the intended character of a building.

Office areas should promote efficient utilization of land near transit stops. These FARS encourage multi-story buildings and structured parking whenever possible. Larger office areas should be located in Urban TODS to create a major focus of symbiotic uses. Smaller, local-serving office areas create opportunities for small businesses in close proximity to retail and transit. Professional offices with resident-serving uses should be given priority in location.

Core Commercial Configuration

The configuration of shops in the core area must balance pedestrian and auto comfort, visibility, and accessibility. While anchor stores may need to orient to an arterial and parking lots, smaller shops should orient to pedestrian "Main Streets" and plazas. Direct local street access from the local neighborhood is required.

The typical form of a suburban retail center is oriented entirely to the auto and parking. Smaller shops are dependent on their relationship to the anchor stores when arrival is only by car. TODS offer the opportunity for a more diverse patronage, both from the traditional auto/anchor and from the walk-in neighborhood and transit activity. To attract foot traffic to local shops, the configuration of streets, entrances, and parking must provide a comfortable route for pedestrians. Traversing large parking lots and access roads designed for heavy auto traffic will discourage them. Configurations which provide traditional "Main Street" sidewalk storefronts in combination with arterial-oriented anchors can provide for both pedestrians and auto accessibility.

Core commercial areas should be configured to allow standard parking quantities, access, and visibility for the car, as well as a convenient path for local pedestrians. Often, the smaller shops

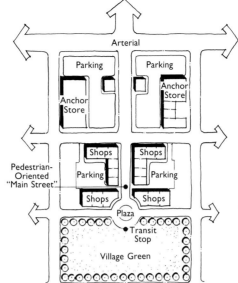

can turn to form a pedestrian-oriented "Main Street" with streetside parking and rear parking lots. This "Main Street" forms a pleasant place to walk, and should connect the residential areas and parks with the shops and transit stop. Simultaneously, the edge of the core area fronting the arterial may house larger parking areas and anchor stores in locations visible from arterials. Anchor stores, such as supermarkets and drug stores, are encouraged to provide entries to both their parking lot and the pedestrian-oriented shopping street.

Commercial Building Setbacks

Building setbacks from public streets should be minimized. Setbacks should reflect the desired character of the area and bring buildings close to the sidewalk.

The street and sidewalk is the main pedestrian activity center. Minimal setbacks bring buildings close to the street and the pedestrians. This defined and close edge enlivens commercial areas by encouraging window shopping and streetside activity.

Buildings in core commercial areas should be encouraged to build to the sidewalk edge whenever possible. Anchor tenants in New Growth Areas, such as supermarkets, should not be strictly held to this require-

15-20'
Sidewalk

ment because patrons will tend to use their cars for major grocery shopping trips and anchor tenants often require visible surface parking. Smaller ancillary shops should be brought to the street edge with minimum setbacks. Parking areas and parking garages should be recessed or placed to the rear of buildings when possible. Larger setbacks of no more than 20 feet should be permitted for multi-story office buildings and streetside outdoor cafes and patios in core commercial areas.

Commercial Building Facades

Building facades should be varied and articulated to provide visual interest to pedestrians. Street level windows and numerous building entries are required in the core commercial area. Arcades, porches, bays, and balconies are encouraged. In no case shall the streetside facade of a building consist of an unarticulated blank wall or an unbroken series of garage doors.

Varied and interesting building facades are key to making a place "pedestrian-oriented." Streets with monotonous and unarticulated buildings are not conducive to pedestrian activity and make walking less appealing.

Building designs should provide as much visual stimulus as possible, without creating a chaotic image. Buildings should incorporate design elements at the street level that draw in pedestrians and reinforce street activity.

Streetside buildings should encourage window shopping, heavy foot traffic in and out of stores, and people-watching from outdoor seating areas. Facades should vary from one building to the next, rather than create an overly unified frontage. Building materials such as concrete, masonry, tile, stone, and wood should be encouraged; glass curtain walls and reflective glass should be discouraged.

Commercial Building Entries

Primary ground-floor commercial building entrances may orient to plazas, parks, or pedestrian-oriented streets, not to interior blocks or parking lots. Secondary entries from the interior of a block are also permitted. Anchor tenant retail buildings may have their entries from off-street parking lots; however, on-street entries are strongly encouraged.

The pedestrian life of a building is at its entry. If the entry orients to parking lots, it steals the activity and life from the street, the main pedestrian route, while signaling that auto access is preferred.

Entries into small shops and offices should face directly onto a pedestrian-oriented street. Buildings with multiple retail tenants should have numerous entries to the street; small single-entry malls are discouraged. Off-street parking should also be located at the rear of buildings with "paseos" leading to the street and primary entrances. Handicapped access must be incorporated into the overall commercial area design.

Some retail anchor stores (above 30,000 sq-ft), such as grocery stores, need parking lot access to the primary entry. In these cases, pedestrian access to the entry should also be provided from the street and configured so pedestrians are not required to walk through the parking lot to enter the store. Along walls without entries, building elevations should include windows and display areas, and/or be lined with small retail shops; secondary retail signage along these walls is also permitted.

Upper-Story Uses

Retail developments in the core commercial area may exceed Floor Area Ratio standards by adding additional floors of residential and/or office uses. When using this bonus, the intensity of the retail use must not be reduced. The required amount of retail parking may be reduced while parking for residential units and office space must be added.

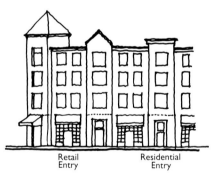

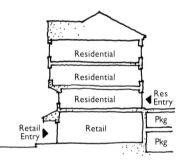

This density bonus for retail buildings is designed as an incentive for developers to provide office and residential uses in the core commercial areas. The amount of upper floor office or residential use may be determined on a site-specific basis through the community plan or specific plan process. Special care must be given to the design of residential units to ensure privacy and security.

Taller buildings are encouraged in the core commercial areas to provide visual interest, a more urban character, street security at night, and to concentrate pedestrian activity. In addition, upper-floor residential and/or office space can support the retail by bringing a greater number of lunch-time and after-work shoppers.

Proximity of Competing Retail

New neighborhood and convenience retail centers should be incorporated into TODs, as much as possible. New competing retail uses should be strictly limited within one mile of the core commercial area.

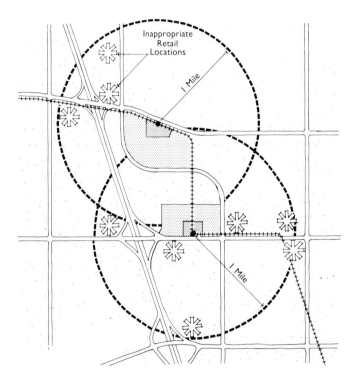

TODs depend on retail uses for a focus and pedestrian destination. Competing centers in locations which do not support transit or pedestrian-oriented neighborhoods can diminish the opportunity to build transit-oriented mixed-use centers. Many General Plans, in fact, significantly overzone for commercial sites, thus diminishing the ability of an area to concentrate retail uses and create activity centers. Each growth area should be examined to determine whether the location of these commercial uses may be in conflict with the goals of promoting transit usage, encouraging walking or biking for some daily trips, and building a network of streets that allows auto users to travel to local shops on local streets.

In order for the core commercial area to attract major anchor tenants and be economically viable, new competing retail centers must be limited through zoning amendments within the TOD's market area. This provides an incentive for development on Redevelopable and Infill Sites and is a key guideline to enable linear areas to function as TODs. Strip commercial uses that extend beyond a 10-minute walking distance of a transit stop should be limited so that businesses that fit into the TOD can capitalize upon their location and proximity to transit.

Residential Areas

Residential Densities

Residential densities within Neighborhood TODs must be a minimum of 7 units per net acre and a minimum average of at least 10 units per net acre. Residential densities within Urban TODs must be a minimum of 12 units per net acre and have a minimum average of at least 15 units per net acre. Maximum densities should be set by local plans.

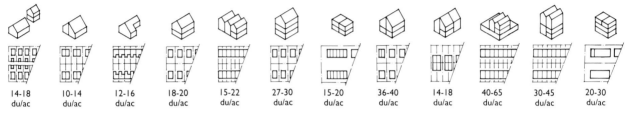

| 14-18 du/ac | 10-14 du/ac | 12-16 du/ac | 18-20 du/ac | 15-22 du/ac | 27-30 du/ac | 15-20 du/ac | 36-40 du/ac | 14-18 du/ac | 40-65 du/ac | 30-45 du/ac | 20-30 du/ac |

The range of permissible densities is designed to encourage transit ridership, as well as provide a variety of housing types. Residential densities are measured in net densities on residential land area. Minimum densities are established to avoid "squandering" valuable transit-accessible land.

Small-lot single-family homes can range from seven to ten units per acre. Single-family homes with ancillary units are feasible between 12 and 17 units per net acre. Ancillary units are calculated as 1 unit per lot. For example, a 4,500 sq-ft or smaller lots will create densities of 16 units/net acre or greater if developed with an ancillary unit. Townhouses can provide between 18 and 29 units per acre. Apartment buildings up to three stories can provide densities of 35-50 du/net acre. Actual densities should strike a balance between emphasizing the impor-tance of development around transit stops and blending in with existing surrounding neighborhoods.

The required "minimum average" density requirement allows flexibility to respond to changing market conditions and encourages a mix of housing types. The range of permissible residential densities which can be combined to achieve this "minimum average" density is broad, with its maximum determined by the nature of the surrounding community.

Ancillary Units

Ancillary "granny" units are encouraged to increase affordability and diversity. These units should be located in the single-family portion of residential areas. The additional unit will be counted toward meeting the minimum average density requirement.

Ancillary units, or second units, create affordable rental units without changing the character and quality of single-family areas. They can also serve to offset housing costs for the primary unit, provide needed space for a teenager or elderly family member, or act as transitional single-family housing. Ancillary units can be provided in residential areas, either as part of the primary home or above a garage. At least one off-street parking space is required for the ancillary unit. Development fees should be waived in recognition of the larger benefits provided by this type of housing.

Ancillary units will be calculated as an additional unit per lot. The following table illustrates the resulting density when ancillary units are provided.

LOCATION	LOT SIZE	NET DENSITY WITHOUT SECOND UNIT	NET DENSITY WITH SECOND UNIT
TOD	33' x 100'	11 u/ac	22 u/ac
TOD	40' x 100'	9 u/ac	18 u/ac
TOD	45' x 100'	8 u/ac	16 u/ac
Secondary Area	50' x 100'	7 u/ac	14 u/ac
Secondary Area	65' x 100'	5 u/ac	10 u/ac

Ancillary units are strongly encouraged to provide rental housing opportunities and to meet the increasing demand for a variety of housing types. They also increase the density of an area without changing the pattern of single-lot private ownership which traditionally has a very strong market. As a source of affordable rental housing they avoid the "institutional" character of many apartment projects and the segregation of low-income groups.

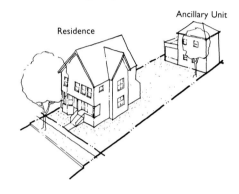

Residence   Ancillary Unit

Residential Building Setbacks

Residential building setbacks from public streets should be minimized, while maintaining privacy. Minimum and maximum front setbacks should be established that reflect the desired character of an area and ensure that residences address streets and sidewalks.

In most new residential areas, building setbacks should be between 10 and 15 feet from the property line at the sidewalk; in Redevelopable Areas and Infill Sites, residential setbacks should complement the setback of surrounding buildings. Where units are set above finished grade, such as over depressed parking garages, the setback may be reduced. If housing occurs over first-floor commercial space, no setback is required. Porches, bays, and balconies should be allowed

to project into these setbacks to contribute to a street's human scale and activity. If residential units are set back from the street, the area should be landscaped.

In residential areas, minimal front yard setbacks encourage recessed garages and dedicate a greater portion of the lot to private back yards. Reduced setbacks also create safer and more active streets. Residents can more easily watch over the street and know their neighbors.

Residential Building Facades

Building facades should be varied and articulated to provide visual interest to pedestrians. Frequent building entries and windows should face the street. Front porches, bays, and balconies are encouraged. In no case shall a facade of a building consist of an unarticulated blank wall or an unbroken series of garage doors.

Varied and human-scaled building facades are key to making a place "pedestrian-oriented." Building designs should provide a high level of visual interest, without creating a chaotic image. Residences should include design elements that enhance the streetscape and address the street. Porches and bays should face the street. Facades should vary from one building to the next to avoid a monotonous streetscape.

Varied and human-scaled facades enhance pedestrians' visual interest and sense of security along streets. Streets with monotonous and unarticulated building frontages make walking less appealing and are not conducive to pedestrian activity. Front porches are the semi-private spaces that create opportunities for social interaction within a neighborhood and bring eyes onto the street, rather than isolating communities behind garage doors.

Residential Building Entries

Primary ground floor residential entries to multi-family buildings must orient to streets, not to interior blocks or parking lots. Secondary and upper-floor entries from the interior of a block are acceptable. The front door to single-family homes, duplexes, and townhouses must be visible from the street.

In residential areas, the front door and guest entry should orient to the street. Private backdoor entries can provide access from alleys, garages, and parking lots. A single security entry from an interior courtyard is permitted if additional entries are provided from the street. Ancillary units and upper-floor units in multi-family or apart-

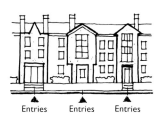

Entries   Entries   Entries

ment complexes may be accessed by rear entries.

As with commercial uses, residential entries should face the street to encourage public activity and to welcome visitors from the on-street guest parking. Housing which "turns its back" on the street destroys the conviviality and safety of a neighborhood.

Entry

Residential Garages

Residential garages should be positioned to reduce their visual impact on the street. This will allow the active, visually interesting features of the house to dominate the streetscape. At a minimum, the garage should be set behind the front facade of the residential building. In single-family areas, garages may be sited in several ways: in the rear accessed from an alley, in the rear accessed by a side drive, or to the side recessed behind the front facade by at least 5 feet.

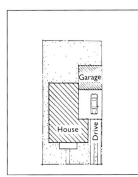

SIDE DRIVE (ATTACHED)

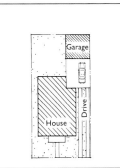

SIDE DRIVE (DETACHED)

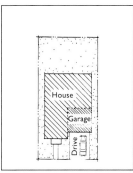

RECESSED FRONT GARAGE

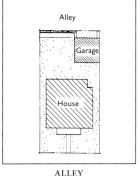

ALLEY
(ATTACHED OR DETACHED)

An active, pleasant, and safe pedestrian environment is created along streets when residences face the street directly. By recessing garages, more active living areas can overlook the street, allowing residents to keep a watchful eye on playing children and participate in neighborhood activity. This configuration also creates a more human-scaled and less monotonous environment by minimizing the visual impact of large, blank garage doors and by enclosing the street with a variety of architectural elements, such as windows, bays, and porches.

Garages must be sited away from the street, behind or below residential buildings. Where the garage is below residences, it should be depressed so that the first floor of living units is not more than about four feet above finished grade. Tandem parking is permitted and encouraged in garages.

Secondary Areas

Types and Proximity of Secondary Areas

There are three types of Secondary Areas: 1) those separated by an arterial but close to the transit stop; 2) those separated by the arterial but further from the transit stop; and 3) those of greater distance but without arterial separation. Secondary Areas located across an arterial, but in close proximity to the center, may be best suited for large-scale employment, while those further from the core area should provide low-density residential housing. Those with direct adjacency should provide low-density housing, public schools, and community parks.

Secondary Areas provide an important support base for both the core commercial area and transit ridership. They also provide opportunities for low-density residential development and large employment sites. If properly designed, Secondary Areas can reinforce the viability of the TOD and provide sites for land-intensive uses such as school sites, open space, and large community parks, as well as major employment too large to fit in the TOD.

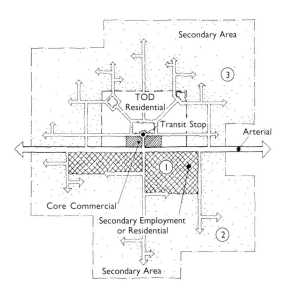

The variety of uses possible within Secondary Areas should be placed in appropriate locations. Large employment sites should be located directly across the arterial from the transit and commercial core. Schools should be located for easy pedestrian access from all residential areas. Parks should be distributed within each neighborhood. Small convenience retail shops can help create neighborhood sub-centers along with parks and daycare facilities.

Residential Quantities and Densities in Secondary Areas

The proportion of single-family to multi-family housing within a growth area should approximate demand based on local income and demographic trends. The minimum average residential density within Secondary Areas should be 6 units per net acre. Ancillary units will be counted as an additional unit per lot.

Secondary Areas provide opportunities for low-density housing types that should not be accommodated in TODs but are essential to ensuring diversity and choice. Secondary Areas also provide housing for the "move up" market and for larger families which still seek the advantages of proximity to the TOD. In some regions, such as Portland, goals are adopted to achieve a 50%/50% split between single-family and multi-family housing. On average throughout the country, however, the split is closer to 60% single-family 40% multi-family. In other areas, a 70%/30% ratio may be more appropriate. Regional and sub-regional household income, age, and size trends should be used to establish the most appropriate ratio target goals.

A variety of low-density housing types and densities should be provided in Secondary Areas such that a minimum average density of 6 units per net acre is maintained. To help meet this minimum average density, higher-density half-plexes and duplexes may be located on street corners or ancillary units could be provided. Custom houses at three units per acre can be balanced with small-lot single-family units with granny flats.

Non-Residential Uses in Secondary Areas

Those parts of Secondary Areas that are closest to the TOD may have select employment-generating uses and/or park-and-ride lots to complement the transit and commercial center. Daycare, neighborhood parks, schools, small convenience stores, and public recreation facilities may also be combined to create neighborhood subcenters in Secondary Areas.

Secondary Areas should contain uses that support the TOD, but do not compete with the major retail, professional office, service commercial, and public uses in the core commercial area. In most cases, Secondary Areas will primarily comprise of low-density single-family neighborhoods and parks. In limited cases, large single-use offices or light industrial uses with sufficient employment density to support transit may be located across the arterial from the core commercial area. These uses must generate an equal or greater number of persons per acre as generated by residential uses at a density of 7 dwelling units per net acre (approximately 16 persons/acre). For example, a typical office development will generate between 30 and 40 employees/acre, while a standard industrial development only generates 10 to 15 employees per acre. A mix of these employment types would be appropriate for a close-in

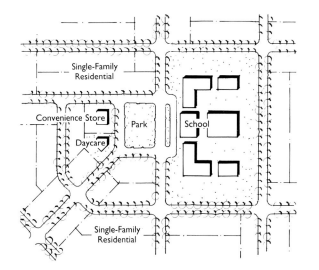

Secondary Area, but low intensity light industrial uses would not be considered transit-supportive.

Neighborhood parks, daycare, schools, and small convenience retail shops should be distributed throughout the Secondary Area to provide focus and identity for sub-areas. These sub-centers should not compete with the central commercial center but can provide a recreation and convenience destination within walking distance of each home. They should be organized to focus individual neighborhoods.

Schools and large community parks are important elements shared by both the Secondary Area and the TOD. They should be located to provide easy, non-arterial access to all the resi-dential areas, most easily accomplished at the edge between Secondary Area and TOD. They should also be used as part of the bike and pedestrian linkage between the two areas.

Streets and Bikeways in Secondary Areas

The primary roadway system in Secondary Areas must provide strong, direct connections to the TOD core commercial area and transit stop. Neighborhood streets should provide non-segregated bikeways while central "connector" streets should provide marked bike lanes.

The street system within a Secondary Area differs from typical single-family areas, because its street system allows direct access to the TOD and its commercial area without use of an arterial. In contrast, most subdivision streets lead to collector streets and then to arterials as the only access to local destinations. A series of smaller "connector streets" that are pedestrian- and bike-friendly should provide direct access to the center. Multiple connector streets will have slower auto speeds and smaller traffic volumes because the streets are narrow and because traffic is dispersed over several routes.

Because of the distances, bicycles are one of the most likely modes of travel for Secondary Area residents who are apt to use public transit. Strong bicycle connections that follow the shortest possible routes will provide additional encouragement for Secondary Area residents to use transit. Arterials and selected connector roadways in Secondary Areas must provide safe, separated or marked bicycle lanes allowing quick travel to the transit stop. Secondary Area bicycle paths should connect with the TOD bicycle system.

Parks, Plazas, and Civic Buildings

Location of Parks and Plazas

Parks and plazas should provide a public focus for each neighborhood. They should be located next to public streets, residential areas, and retail uses. Parks should not be formed from residual areas, used as buffers to surrounding developments, or used to separate buildings from streets.

Public parks and plazas are fundamental features of livable and enjoyable higher-density communities. Parks and plazas in TODs act as neighborhood meeting places, recreational activity centers, childcare facilities, and lunch time picnic spots. Because their function is primarily "public activity," they are most appropriately located central to residential or core areas.

Park and plaza sites should reinforce retail and residential areas by creating places suitable for informal gatherings or public events. Appropriate sites are centrally located and adjacent to streets and shopping areas. In many communities, parks and plazas are located on sites that are not suitable for other types of uses, such as under freeways, on oddly shaped parcels at the edge of a development, or within private residential or office complexes. These sites are not appropriate for public parks and plazas and rarely function effectively as such.

Size and Frequency of Parks

Parks should be developed throughout TODs and surrounding Secondary Areas to meet on-site population needs. One- to four-acre village parks should be placed within two blocks of any residence. Five- to ten-acre neighborhood parks with large playing fields should be located at the edge of the TOD or adjacent to schools. Ten- to thirty-acre community parks should be placed along regional open space or bicycle networks. Total park acreage should be based on the quantity of residential development and/or equivalent to roughly 5 to 10% of the site area.

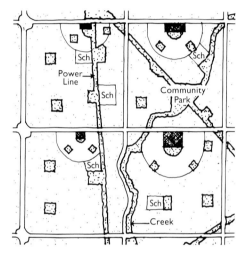

Small and frequent parks should be dispersed throughout residential areas to provide auto-free destinations for children within a TOD. Too often, parks are aggregated for marginal savings in maintenance costs, and become too remote to be safe for foot or bike access. One- to four-acre sites can easily accommodate a useful range of active and passive uses for a variety of age groups. Basketball, tennis, tot lots, picnic areas, gardens, and strolling areas are feasible at this scale. With two acres (a typical city block) a softball field with other facilities is possible. These smaller parks are also safer; they are shallow enough for street and residential surveillance and they easily become the informal responsibility of local residents.

To preserve the compact, mixed-use character of TODs, larger parks and playfields should be located in Secondary Areas. Mid-sized neighborhood parks, with their soccer, baseball, and football fields, are often successfully placed next to elementary and middle schools, where active play areas can be jointly used and evening lights and occasional crowds can be managed. Their size reflects the needs of a large residential population and therefore they are typically shared by a TOD and its Secondary Area.

Many cities are now planning for very large "community parks." These 10- to 30-acre parks tend to serve populations of 15,000 or more and should be strategically placed to provide easy access for the broader community along both street and bicycle networks. Open space features, such as creeks, rivers, knolls, and woodlands, can be incorporated as park amenities.

The standards for the ratio of park area to number of residents varies widely from city to city. A minimum of 3.5 acres per thousand population is advisable in TODs, as parks enhance the quality of the public domain, create more convenient recreation areas, and provide open space for moderate- to high-density housing.

Village Greens and Transit Plazas

Village greens and transit plazas may be used to create a prominent civic component to core commercial areas. Village greens should be between 1 and 3 acres in size; transit plazas may be smaller. They should be placed at the juncture between the core commercial area and surrounding residential or office uses.

In most communities, the traditional "commons" has been lost to auto-dominated shopping centers and park-and-ride lots. Village greens, where workers meet during lunch time and shoppers see their neighbors, are rarely considered in modern suburbia. This essential piece of the commons once gave identity to the larger community and acted as the physical glue between residential neighborhoods, commercial centers, and civic services.

A central public space may be used to reintroduce the public realm into the core commercial area. Village greens and transit plazas should be placed adjacent to retail shops or the transit stop. Their character should vary based on their size, function, and purpose. In some cases, public buildings, such as a town hall or daycare facility, may be placed within a village green. Transit plazas may incorporate "kiss-n-ride" drop-off zones, but should not be separated from the transit stop itself. Clear pedestrian access must be provided from the green or plaza to surrounding employment and residential areas.

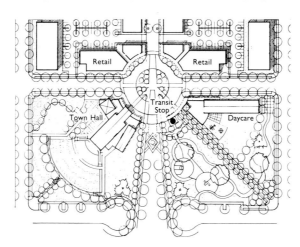

Park and Plaza Design

Public parks and plazas should be designed for both active and passive uses. They should reflect and reinforce the character of the surrounding area and accommodate the anticipated intensity of use. Their form should be coherent and memorable, rather than residual. Their design should respect vistas created by streets. Plant types must reflect the local climate and history.

Various types of parks and plazas can be designed to establish an identity or character for each neighborhood. For example, plazas in commercial core areas may be most appropriately designed with finished hardscape materials such as stone or brick, and include fountains and seating areas; parks in residential areas could be developed with grassy fields, play equipment, and

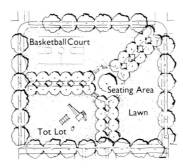

sports facilities. Parks should not be situated on oddly shaped parcels or within private areas.

Because parks and plazas will be focal points of neighborhood activity, special consideration should be given to making these public spaces not only functionally appropriate, but consistent with the character and density of the surrounding area. Sensitive integration of public spaces is also critical to public acceptance and commercial success.

Park and plaza landscaping should provide trees and plants that make comfortable, relaxing environments. The amount and location of such landscaping should be appropriate to and complement the character and design of the space. Landscaping should allow comfortable use in both summer and winter months.

Because parks and plazas form the spine of urban public spaces, views and linkages to streets and other public spaces and buildings must be respected and reinforced through design elements. For example, paths should align with important viewpoints; trees should not block views of significant public monuments or buildings; and perimeter landscaping should allow views into a park.

Public park and plaza landscaping should create places that are comfortable, safe, and linked with the overall network of public spaces. Flexible landscaping guidelines should be permitted so that a variety of spaces are created which reflect the role and character of the place.

Community Buildings

Civic services, such as community buildings, government offices, recreation centers, post offices, libraries, and daycare, should be placed in central locations as highly visible focal points. Where feasible, they should be close to the transit stop.

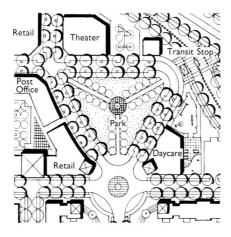

The re-integration of our civic and commercial world is essential to creating strong communities. Daycare, libraries, police and fire stations, and post offices should be located with retail areas or adjacent to village greens. Daycare should also be located in association with major neighborhood parks in Secondary Areas to contribute to the sense of identity of single-family neighborhoods.

Community buildings can enhance the identity of an area, as well as reinforce connections with the past in older neighborhoods. Civic structures will contribute to the level of activity in TOD commercial centers and encourage walking and transit use by patrons and employees. Community buildings associated with parks can contribute to the identifying aspects of Secondary Area neighborhoods, as well. These parks and community buildings will help to differentiate one neighborhood from the next, and help to create a node of activity apart from the core area.

The architectural quality of community buildings can elevate their prominence and civic importance. Major building entries should face public streets and be strongly articulated. Massing and architectural features should be designed to take advantage of vistas along streets to visually connect these civic buildings with their surrounding neighborhood. Major public buildings should have a civic presence enhanced by their height, mass, and materials. The architecture should convey a sense of permanence and importance.

Schools and Community Parks

If needed, school sites and community parks should be located at the edges of TODs within Secondary Areas. Strong pedestrian and bike links should connect these sites with the commercial and transit core.

While schools and community parks are not necessary appropriate uses within the TOD, they may be needed to serve the larger population. Schools and community parks should be located within convenient walking distance of the TOD, along pedestrian paths, streets, and bikeways which follow the shortest route to the commercial and transit core.

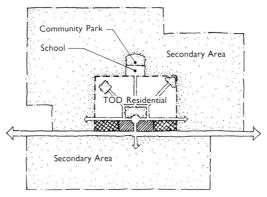

Studies of travel behavior indicate that roughly half of all daily trips are to local destinations, such as schools, recreation, and shopping. If only a portion of those trips were made on foot or bike, the reduction of vehicle miles traveled would be significant. This further supports the importance of providing safe and direct street and bicycle routes for children.

Daycare

Sites for pre-school daycare facilities should be provided in all TODs and Secondary Areas. They should be located en route to transit or within the core commercial area.

More households are and will be headed by double-income or single parents, creating a strong demand for childcare services. A basic objective is to provide housing opportunities for a variety of household types, and daycare facilities are increasingly a necessary daily part of residents' lives. Additionally, many parents now lengthen early morning and evening auto trips by driving to a childcare facility before continuing on to work. Locating childcare facilities in TODs will not only provide a necessary service, but will allow parents to make the daycare

trip part of their transit commute trip, thus reducing vehicle miles traveled.

Daycare facilities should be convenient and accessible to local residents and employees. Sites should be located within residential neighborhoods, adjacent to parks, core commercial areas, and office buildings. The precise parcel size and size of the facility should be determined in conjunction with appropriate local agencies. Daycare facilities for school-age children should be located at school sites to meet the needs of each school's students.

Street and Circulation System

Street Dimensions and Design Speeds

Street widths, design speeds, and number of travel lanes should be minimized without compromising auto safety, on-street parking, or bike access. Streets should be designed for travel speeds of 15 miles per hour. Travel lanes should be 8 to 10 feet wide.

The street network should create a safer, more comfortable pedestrian and bicycling environment. Narrower streets slow traffic and reduce accidents by requiring the driver to be cautious.

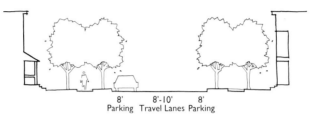

8'
Parking   8'-10'
Travel Lanes   8'
Parking

Local and "connector" streets should be designed or redesigned such that lane widths, design speeds, and number of travel lanes are kept to a minimum – without compromising auto safety. This will help provide space for landscaping, bicycle access and on-street parking.

Minimum street dimensions are intended to make streets more intimate in scale while providing for municipal service vehicle access. In areas where local streets already exist, street widths should be evaluated to determine if improvements could be made to narrow pavement width, yet maintain safety. Smaller street sections will also reduce crosswalk dimensions and result in cost savings which can in turn be allocated for pedestrian amenities. Slower design speeds will help keep traffic in residential areas moving slowly and safely. A high design speed often results in the broad, curving street configurations that invite drivers to exceed speed limits. Within the quarter mile of the TOD there is no reason for, or significant time saved by, traveling faster than fifteen miles per hour.

Street Vistas

Where possible, streets should frame vistas of the core area, public buildings, parks, and natural features.

Streets that frame vistas will establish a series of pedestrian "landmarks" to help make the community spatially memorable. Streets should be designed so they terminate at important buildings and places. Straight streets, in particular, allow clear views to landmarks and are encouraged. In areas with steep slopes, the street system should work

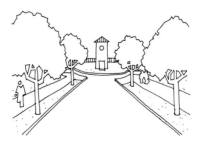

with the natural topography to accent important landmarks.

Visible landmarks help orient pedestrians and make walking routes interesting and memorable. Straight streets make destinations more accessible by making them visible; if a destination is visible, a person is more likely to walk to it.

Street Trees

Shade trees are required along all streets. Street trees should be spaced no further than 30 feet on center in planter strips or tree wells located between the curb and sidewalk. Tree species and planting techniques should be selected to create a unified image for the street, provide an effective canopy, avoid sidewalk damage, and minimize water consumption.

Many streets are identified and remembered by their street trees. Streets should be lined with a limited selection of trees to give them a unified and distinct image. Adequate sight distances must be maintained in order to ensure safety. Within TODs, trees should be placed in a planter strip or tree well between the street and sidewalk. In Secondary Areas that do not have planter strips, the trees should be kept close to the sidewalk to provide shade and should be aligned to visu-

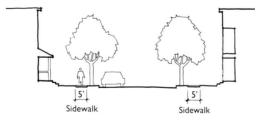

ally frame the street. In all cases, trees should be trimmed regularly to accommodate buses and service vehicles. Tree maintenance should be ensured through the creation of Landscape Maintenance Districts or other means.

Shade for the comfort of the pedestrian is key to creating a viable walking environment. Street trees help reduce heat build-up from large asphalt areas and create a cooler micro-climate. Trees also provide habitat for local birds and help create a beautiful community.

Sidewalks

Sidewalks are required on all streets and must provide an unobstructed path at least 5 feet wide. Larger sidewalk dimensions are desirable in core commercial areas where pedestrian activity will be greatest and where outdoor seating is encouraged.

Comfortable sidewalks reinforce pedestrian environments. The comfort and convenience of the pedestrian trip will reduce internal auto trips and reinforce the efficiency of the transit system by creating destinations which are attainable without a car and origins which do not depend solely on park-and-ride mode transfers.

Many communities have discontinuous sidewalks. Plans must ensure that sidewalk improvements are pro-vided throughout and constructed in a coordinated manner. A 5-foot clear corridor is a minimum width for two people to walk abreast comfortably. Larger sidewalk dimensions are desirable in the core commercial area where pedestrian activity will be greatest and where outdoor seating is encouraged. Generally, sidewalks should be between 5 and 10 feet wide in TODs; width should be determined based on location, context and role within the area.

On-Street Parking

On-street parking is encouraged on all streets, except arterials. On Redevelopable and Infill Sites, existing streets should be modified, as feasible, to provide on-street parking and landscaping. Parking lanes should be seven to eight feet wide.

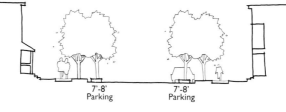

7'-8' Parking   7'-8' Parking

Streetside parking is critical to keeping the focus of a community on the street, rather than on the interior of lots. On-street parking helps to create street activity, as well as provide functional spaces. It supports orienting building entries to the street by providing convenient access for guests and patrons. Parallel parking should be used most often; however, angled on-street parking is encouraged along shopping streets within core commercial areas, where slow drive-by traffic is desired. To maintain travel speeds and emergency vehicle access, on-street parking should not be permitted on arterials.

On-street parking on local streets can also be compatible with bicycle travel, provided that auto speeds are slow enough (15 to 20 miles per hour) to allow bikers to travel in the street at the same speed as the cars. However, on selected high-volume connector streets where on-street parking is to be retained, it is desirable to include sufficient room within the roadway for bike lanes.

On-street parking helps to "civilize" the street for pedestrians by creating a buffer between moving cars and the sidewalk. The additional parking helps to replace areas devoted to large off-street surface parking lots and places the parking near the desired street-side building entries. On-street parking tends to slow the flow of through traffic and helps to develop a pedestrian environment where walking is desired.

Intersection Design

Intersections should be designed to facilitate both pedestrian and vehicular movement. Intersection dimensions should be minimized while providing adequate levels of service.

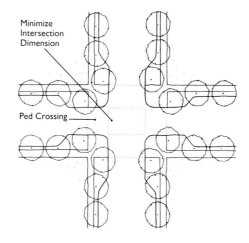

Minimize Intersection Dimension

Ped Crossing

Since the TOD street is conceived as more than a conduit for cars, street and intersection widths should be kept to a minimum. Intersections should be designed to slow traffic and to reduce pedestrian crossing distances. Unless absolutely necessary for facilitating safety, right and left turn lanes at intersections should be avoided.

A street system should balance the needs and viability of the pedestrian, as well as the car. Reduced auto speeds improve pedestrian accessibility and safety, and can continue to accommodate safe vehicular movement. Minimum curb radius at the intersection will reduce the pedestrian crossing distance while reducing the speed of the car through the intersection.

Retrofit of Existing Streets
for Pedestrian and Auto Connections

Existing on-site pedestrian, bike, parking, and auto circulation systems should be redesigned to encourage pedestrian/bike access between uses, public spaces and Secondary Areas.

Every effort should be made to encourage and facilitate pedestrian access at sites that are redeveloped into TODs. In some cases this may require redesigning existing streets and pedestrian systems. Connections between TODs and surrounding areas are vital to providing all of the advantages that a walkable, mixed-use, and transit-oriented development can provide.

On sites that will be retrofitted or redeveloped into TODs, existing roadways and pedestrian networks may need to be redesigned to facilitate pedestrian access between buildings and transit, regardless of parcelization patterns. Connections to the core and transit, and be-

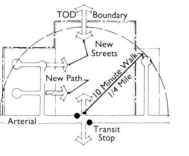

tween the TOD and surrounding areas, are especially critical. Improvements should be made to open walking paths between uses, to protect important vistas, to connect with existing trail systems, and to slow auto traffic. Handicapped access strategies should be incorporated into all street and pathway retrofits. In auto-oriented suburban areas, pedestrian access may be improved by opening key cul-de-sacs to foot and bicycle traffic. In areas dominated by "superblocks," new internal streets should be built to provide pedestrian-friendly connections to workplaces and other destinations.

Arterial Streets and Thoroughfares

Arterial streets and thoroughfares should allow efficient conveyance of through traffic and must not pass through TODs – they are a barrier to pedestrians. Portions of Secondary Areas may be located across an arterial from a TOD.

The regional traffic circulation system is dependent upon an efficient and smooth-flowing network of arterial and thoroughfare streets. Traffic on arterial streets should not be slowed by activity in the TOD. TOD sites should be selected such that arterial and thoroughfare streets are located at the TOD's periphery, not through its center.

In many communities, the main spine of the transit system will follow arterial streets and major thoroughfares. These four- to six-lane streets are barriers to pedestrian activity and thus should not be the focal point for the TOD. If possible

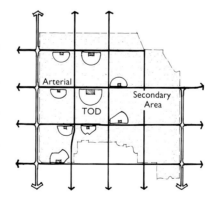

the transit stop should be located within the site or at least to one side of the arterial.

Arterials may be located between the TOD and the Secondary Area. The lower-intensity uses in the Secondary Area can benefit from proximity to the core commercial area, permitting workers and bicyclists access to daily services. Convenient pedestrian and bike crossings should be provided wherever cross-arterial connections are made, providing on-demand pedestrian-activated signals. Under- and over-crossings are expensive and generally unused; they are discouraged unless absolutely necessary in already developed areas.

Connector Streets

"Connector" streets should provide linkages within TODs and Secondary Areas to core commercial areas, schools, and community parks without requiring the use of arterials. They should be designed to carry moderate levels of local traffic smoothly, in a way that is compatible with bicycle and foot traffic. A network of connectors should provide several alternative paths through neighborhoods to the center. The connector network should not provide a through-route alternative to arterials.

Rather than the current system of "collector" streets which focus traffic and direct it to the arterial, "connectors" provide multiple routes to local destinations. Connector streets should form a network of routes that provide alternative paths through neighborhoods and to major destinations, such as core commercial areas, transit stops, schools, and parks.

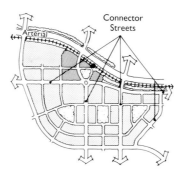

Connectors are intended to carry moderate levels of local traffic from neighborhoods to arterials and major destinations. Their design and alignment should balance efficient vehicular travel with the safety and livability of residential areas. Providing a connector network with frequent, alternative paths will distribute traffic volumes over more routes. The resulting trip distribution will permit connectors to be lined with residences and provide an en-vironment oriented towards pedestrians and bicyclists. "T" intersections and "dog leg" alignments should be used to reduce through traffic and reduce speeds. The width of connector streets should be minimized, especially where traffic volumes are not high.

On-street parking should be provided. Connectors should include bikeways where bicyclists share the street with a delineated bike lane. Unlike the back yards and soundwalls of collector streets, houses should front onto connector streets. Driveway cuts should be minimized and alley access to rear gara-ges encouraged, to minimize potential conflicts among autos and bicyclists, and for the convenience of residents along connectors. Connectors should be aligned along the edge of parks and open spaces to enhance the character of the route.

Commercial Streets

Commercial streets located in the center of core commercial areas should be designed to accommodate pedestrians, slow traffic, provide on-street parking, and create pleasant shopping environments.

Commercial streets can create a pleasant and active commercial spine within core commercial areas. Slow traffic and comfortable pedestrian environments will encourage walking for many shopping trips, thereby reducing reliance on the automobile and creating an active "Main Street."

Commercial streets should have two travel lanes and on-street parking in order to create an intimate shopping environment that maintains drive-by visibility to stores. Wider sidewalks, limited curb cuts, street trees, awnings, and arcades should be used to accommodate this active, pedestrian environment. Shops should front onto commercial streets with minimal setbacks.

Local Streets

Local streets should have travel and parking lanes sufficiently narrow to slow traffic and allow trees to form a pleasing canopy over the street, while providing for adequate access for automobiles and service vehicles.

Local streets should be designed to serve low volumes of traffic through a pedestrian-oriented environment. Travel and parking lanes should only be wide enough to allow two vehicles to slowly pass each other. Emergency and service vehicles may use both travel lanes. Parking on each side of the street serves to slow traffic and provide a physical barrier for the pedestrian. Bicycles are encouraged in the street, rather than on separated bikeways. Street trees should be provided to enhance the quality of the neighborhood and provide relief from summer heat.

Local streets are the public open space in which children often play and around which neighbors interact. Vehicular movement should be controlled and provided for within this context. Too often the cul-de-sac is used to achieve the same ends of slower traffic and safety.

Alleys

Where possible, alleys should be used to serve residential and commercial uses within TODs, they are particularly appropriate for lots facing onto parks and connector streets in Secondary Areas.

In areas where walking is to be encouraged, streets lined with garages are undesirable. Alleys provide an opportunity to put the garage to the rear, allowing the more "social" aspects of the home to front the street. Streets lined with porches, entries and living spaces are safer because of this visual surveillance. Alleys in commercial areas place service vehicle access and parking away from the street and sidewalks, affording a more interesting and comfortable streetscape.

Alleys provide relief to the street system and a secondary access to individual parcels. Alley-accessed garages relieve the street side of the house from being dominated by garage doors and cramped by curb cuts. Design of alleys should provide sufficient lighting to ensure night-time safety; ancillary housing units facing onto alleys should be provided adequate parking. Where alleys intersect with streets, adequate sight distances and building setbacks should be provided.

Pedestrian and Bicycle System

Pedestrian Routes

Pedestrian routes should be located along or visible from all streets. They must provide clear, comfortable, and direct access to the core commercial area and transit stop. Primary pedestrian routes and bikeways should be bordered by residential fronts, public parks, plazas, or commercial uses. Where street connections are not feasible, short pedestrian paths can provide connections between residential and retail areas. Routes through parking lots or at the rear of residential developments should be avoided.

Too often pedestrian paths have been separated from streets, giving a confusing message to pedestrians. This can be dangerous because these routes lack adequate surveillance and auto access. The primary pedestrian path system should coincide with the street system. Where a street connection is not feasible, pedestrian connections can be made at the end of cul-de-sacs and by providing passageways through walls surrounding commercial centers.

Paths through parking lots and away from streets should be avoided. Alternate routes around parks should be provided for night use. Safe pedestrian crossings across arterials should be provided where major pedestrian movement is anticipated. On-demand pedestrian signals should be provided during off-peak hours in these locations.

Although the street and sidewalk system will accommodate many destinations, the primary destination will be the commercial core and transit stop. Direct paths to the transit stop should be lined with activities and be shaded. The configuration of parking, shopping, and pedestrian routes should reinforce access to transit.

Up to 75 percent of all household trips are non-job related. Many of these non-commute trips can be captured within the TOD or within a short transit connection. Combining retail uses with a transit stop provides the opportunity for people to accomplish several tasks with one trip. Interruptions in the path and inconvenient walking routes discourage pedestrian travel for these types of trips. Pedestrian access is critical to the displacement of auto trips and to encourage as much transit use as possible.

Arterial Crossings and Pedestrian Bridges

Crosswalks should be provided at all signalized arterial intersections. Under-crossings or bridges designed for pedestrians and bicyclists are discouraged, unless necessary in already developed areas to solve critical access problems.

Crosswalks at signalized intersections should provide easy and safe pedestrian and bicycle movement across arterials or to difficult-to-reach transit stops. On-demand signals can be located at strategic intersections, such as where a connection would be made to a transit stop or core commercial area, which could be activated during off-peak commute hours. Underpasses or pedestrian bridges are discouraged because they are expensive and are generally long, circuitous routes that are often unused. However, in some limited cases, where existing development patterns prevent any other convenient street

crossings, an under- or overpass may be appropriate; direct stairs in addition to handicapped access ramps could be provided to shorten walking distances.

Pedestrians and bicyclists must be permitted to move easily and safely across arterials if an environment that is not reliant on the automobile is to be created. Intersections should be designed to provide direct pedestrian and bicycle connections between core commercial areas, employment areas, parks, schools, residential areas, and other destinations.

Bikeways

A coordinated system of bikeways should be provided in conjunction with TODs or a series of TODs. Important destinations, such as core commercial areas, transit stops, employment centers, parks, open spaces, schools, and other community facilities, should be linked by these bike routes.

Biking can be a major alternative to the auto for local trips, trips to the transit stop, or trips to work. Separated or marked bike lanes on several primary routes to the core area will support this alternative, as will the bike paths along greenways between TODs and employment destinations. On smaller streets, bikes sharing the travel lane will help slow cars to speeds more appropriate for residential streets.

Selected routes to the transit stop should provide marked or separated bikeways connecting with the Secondary Areas and other key destinations. Designated bike lanes should be provided on selected

connector streets and a limited number of local streets that converge upon the commercial and transit center. Bicycle routes are encouraged on small residential streets, but designated or marked bike lanes are not required.

Separated bike paths should also be provided along greenways and arterials, and through open space corridors.

Bikeways should be well-identified by bikeway signs that indicate the beginning, end, and route of the bikeway. Clear destination signs should be provided that direct riders to key activity centers, such as shopping areas, transit stops, recreation facilities, schools, and bike parking facilities.

Bike Parking

Bicycle parking facilities must be provided throughout core commercial areas, in office developments, and at transit stops, schools, and parks.

Secure bike lockers are especially important to "bike-and-ride" transit use, as few will leave their bike unattended for a full working day. Bicycle parking facilities include bike racks, "checks," and lockers. Bike racks must be provided at shopping, school, and recreational destinations in TODs and Secondary Areas. More secure bike parking facilities must be provided at all office/employment uses and at major transit stops. Signs indicating the location of bike parking facilities must be clearly posted. Bike parking may be shared between uses, but should be centrally located, easily accessible to building entries, closer to the building than auto parking areas, and visible from streets or parking lots. These facilities should not block pedestrian routes.

Transit System

Transit Line Location

Transit lines must help define the density, location, and quality of growth in a region. They should be located to allow maximum area for new TODs, to access prime Redevelopable or Infill Sites, and to serve existing dense residential and employment centers.

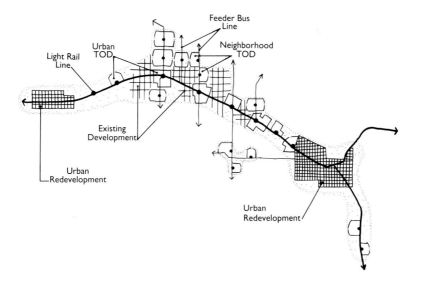

Too often transit lines are located in areas that are not transit-supportive because they have too little density, no pedestrian quality, and little opportunity for redevelopment. Lines through existing suburbs often make this mistake and become dominated by a "park-and-ride" auto access strategy. The alternative is to balance these conditions with alignments that run through New Growth Areas designed for higher densities, mixed-use, and walkability. In more urban areas, neighborhoods which have these qualities should be targeted for new transit, along with areas which could redevelop. Major employment centers, regional destinations, colleges, airports, and cultural facilities are, of course, prime focal points for any system.

A mix of station qualities is important to a successful transit line. Existing railroad or freeway rights-of-way play a large role in determining the routing of fixed-rail transit lines. In some cases this is positive, as is often the case with underutilized freight lines, which can provide sites for redevelopment and infill. Using freeway rights-of-way often precludes sites viable for mixed-use development and comfortable pedestrian access. Where necessary, these freeway alignments can form the logical location for the park-and-ride facilities.

Transit Stop Location

Trunk line transit stops should, whenever possible, be centrally located and adjacent to the core commercial area. Commercial uses should be directly visible and accessible from the transit stop. Feeder bus stops may be located in Secondary Areas along connector streets and adjacent to parks and public facilities.

Accessibility is the key to successful transit ridership. A centrally located transit stop is closest to the greatest number of TOD residents and employees. Transit stops should provide pleasant and convenient access to residential and commercial areas. In the best of all possible worlds the transit station would be in the middle of a TOD, providing the shortest walking distances for all users.

Ideally, the transit stop should be centrally located, away from the arterial, and bus routes should loop through the TOD to the transit stop. If the TOD is to be served by light rail, the line should either feed directly into the heart of the TOD and its core commercial area, or may be located along the arterial street. The core

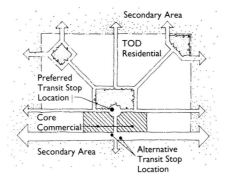

commercial area should be located so that at least a portion of the retail is along the arterial and directly accessible from the transit stop via sidewalks and clear pedestrian connections.

TODs along express and feeder bus routes should respond to the linear nature of the transit line by forming a series of transit-oriented nodes, rather than perpetuating current strip commercial patterns. Where possible, bus routes should follow parallel connector streets that feed directly into the core commercial area, thus helping to separate through traffic and transit operations. Where bus stops must be located along arterials, the TOD should be located on one side with crosswalk improvements to facilitate frequent pedestrian crossings.

Transit Stop Facilities

Comfortable waiting areas, appropriate for year-round weather conditions, must be provided at all transit stops. Passenger drop-off zones should be located close to the stop, but should not interfere with pedestrian access.

At a minimum, transit stops should provide shelter for pedestrians, convenient passenger drop-off zones, telephones, adequate lighting, and secure bike storage. Areas for vendors, small cafes, and other activities useful while waiting are desirable.

Shelters should be designed with passenger safety and comfort in mind. They should be easily recognizable, yet blend with the architecture of the transit station and/or surrounding buildings. Passenger loading zones should be located close to the stop and provide for handicapped access, but should not interfere with the transit stop operations. Secure and safe bicycle storage areas, such as bike lockers, bike racks, or

monitored "bike checks," should also be provided. The frustration caused by the wait for transit can be reduced by creating a lively, inviting, and useful environment at the station. Such activities help populate the station area, increasing safety.

TOD transit stops are apt to be used a greater portion of the year, and by people using a variety of modes to get to them, than are stops in typical auto-oriented developments. Consequently, transit stop facilities should accommodate and encourage active use by providing year-round shelters, convenient loading zones, and secure bike storage.

Access to Transit Stops

Streets must be designed to facilitate safe and comfortable pedestrian crossings to the transit stop. Park-and-ride lots, "kiss-n-ride" and major bus drop-off areas should not isolate the station from local pedestrians.

Most people will use transit only if it is fast, safe, and very convenient. Accessibility to transit stops must be given high priority in the design of streets in order to promote transit ridership. Street crossing placement, design, and markings should recognize the need for fast and flexible access to the stop.

One of the greatest design flaws of station configuration is to surround it with parking and noisy bus areas. This separates the station from the pedestrian and effectively makes the station a detriment to any mixed-use development. Residents rarely enjoy a view of a park-and-ride lot or the noise of a bus zone. These all-too-common configura-

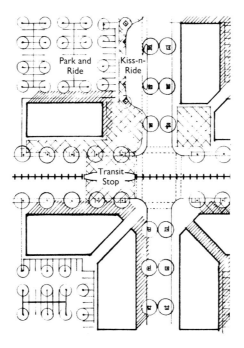

tions destroy the opportunity for an urban environment to evolve in a station area. Often these undesirable facilities can be placed on one side of the station, leaving the other for pedestrian-oriented environments to develop.

Transit passengers are likely to make frequent street crossings, some at mid-block, depending on the location and design of the transit stop. Adjacent street design must recognize the need for easy, safe, and fast pedestrian access, by providing sufficient auto and pedestrian visibility distances, stop signs or manually operated traffic signals, handicapped access, and clearly marked pedestrian crossings at signalized intersections.

Park-and-Ride Lots

Park-and-ride lots are not appropriate for all trunk transit line stops. Surface parking lots specifically devoted to park-and-ride should not be provided in TODs. Rather, they should be located at the ends of trunk lines, at stations with little possibility for mixed-use development, or in Secondary Areas adjacent to the boundaries of TODs. Alternately, park-and-ride lots may be provided within structured parking lots located close to the transit stop.

While park-and-ride lots are extremely important components to building the ridership of the overall transit system, they do not necessarily augment the uses, activities, and densities of a mixed-use, transit-oriented neighborhood. The location and type of park-and-ride lots should be considered in terms of the goals and function of the entire transit system.

Park-and-ride lots are best located adjacent to TODs or at other transit stops. Surface parking lots specifically designed for park-and-ride should be located in close Secondary Areas, just across an arterial, or at the end of the trunk transit line.

Recognizing the need for parking facilities within Urban TODs to serve both the core commercial area and the transit stop, structured parking lots available to the public may be provided. The size of the structured parking facility should be based on projected station and commercial area needs. These parking structures should be financed and constructed in conjunction with other public improvements.

Parking Requirements and Configuration

Parking Standards

Reduced parking standards should be applied to Urban TODs in recognition of their proximity to high frequency transit service, their walkable environment, and mix of uses. Standard parking ratios are recommended for Neighborhood TODs and Secondary Areas.

Limited, rather than ample, parking supplies encourage commuter use of transit service. Minimum requirements help to avoid "spillover" parking in retail areas or nearby neighborhoods; maximums guard against overly generous parking supplies that discourage transit use and contribute to construction of large surface parking lots. The most effective location for implementing reduced parking standards is in Urban TODs located along the trunk transit line network.

For non-residential development, parking standards vary based upon community characteristics such as pedestrian orientation and transit availability. The highest minimum parking requirements are generally found in the newer, more suburban communities as follows:

Office	3.3 spaces/1,000 sq-ft
Retail	5.0 spaces/1,000 sq-ft
Light Industrial	2.5 spaces/1,000 sq-ft

For TODs, reduced *minimum* parking standards should be permitted based on detailed analysis of the conditions in the area. In addition, *maximum* parking ratios should be established for non-residential uses.

Based upon site-specific study, parking requirements should be set approximately within the following ranges:

Office	2-4 spaces/1,000 sq-ft
Retail	3-5 spaces/1,000 sq-ft
Light Industrial	1-3 spaces/1,000 sq-ft

In preparing and implementing a parking ordinance, the following should be taken into consideration:

1. Communities using parking standards which differ from the typical suburban requirements described above should be reviewed to determine the appropriate minimum and maximum standards.

2. Bike parking standards should be established for non-residential uses.

3. Parking studies should be conducted as necessary to evaluate projects that have been granted parking reductions. If recommended by such studies, feasible reductions should be implemented and included as features in future projects.

Joint Use Parking

Joint parking allowances are recommended for adjacent uses with staggered peak periods of demand. Retail, office, and entertainment uses should share parking areas and quantities. A portion of any project's parking requirements may be satisfied by on-street parking.

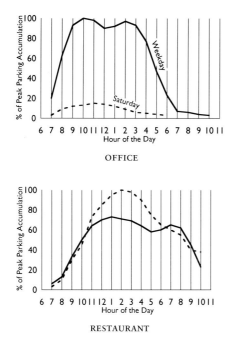

OFFICE

RESTAURANT

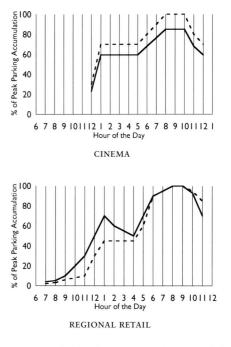

CINEMA

REGIONAL RETAIL

Projects with a mix of uses should seek to reduce the total number of parking spaces by comparing peak demand of each use by time of day, day of the week, and season. Where the varied parking demand for proximate uses allows joint use of a single parking facility, a reduced number of spaces is strongly encouraged. Shared parking areas should be conveniently located to all uses, but do not need to be located on the same parcel as the use.

The complementary relationship between land uses in a mixed-use area encourages multipurpose trips. Thus, a single parking space can serve several land uses. Additionally, peak parking demand for different land uses is often generated at different times during the day, week,

or season. This also allows joint use of the same parking spaces for several uses. Reducing the amount of land devoted to parking allows more efficient use of land closest to transit.

Utilizing on-street parking spaces to fulfill a portion of the total parking requirement will also help reduce the amount of land devoted to parking, while continuing to provide the necessary amount of parking spaces. The number of on-street parking spaces available on the contiguous street frontage of retail, office, or public use sites, may count against the total required number of parking spaces. To ease parking problems, on-site tandem parking is strongly encouraged.

Parking Mitigation Measures

Where reduced parking standards are utilized, mitigation measures should be considered to guard against "spillover" parking impacts. Preferential parking zones should be considered in residential neighborhoods and short-term parking controls may be utilized in core commercial areas.

Where parking ratios are significantly reduced to take advantage of proximity to transit, analysis should be made to determine whether adjacent neighborhoods and shopping areas could be negatively affected by spillover parking during peak hours. Residential parking permits should be considered for neighborhoods; meters or short term parking zones should be considered for shopping areas.

The parking guidelines are intended to not overly restrict parking supply in order to encourage carpooling, bicycling, and transit use. But, in some cases the maximum parking demand for a particular area may be exceeded. Spillover parking can negatively affect surrounding neighborhoods and discourage shopping in commercial areas. Specific projects should be evaluated to determine if mitigation measures would be beneficial.

Parking Configuration

Parking lots should not dominate the frontage of pedestrian-oriented streets, interrupt pedestrian routes, or negatively impact surrounding neighborhoods. Lots should be located behind buildings or in the interior of a block whenever possible. Structured parking is also encouraged and future intensification with structured parking should be considered when designing development plans.

An active pedestrian environment is stimulated by buildings at the sidewalk with numerous entries; surface parking lots are "dead" spaces for pedestrians and drain the life of a street. When possible, parking lots should be placed behind buildings. Since surface parking can

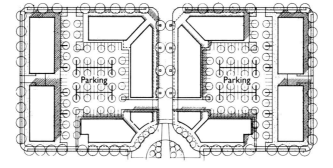

also lower densities and intensities – reducing transit ridership – surface lots should be minimized with structured parking and shared parking.

Parking lots that serve buildings facing pedestrian-oriented streets should be located to the rear of buildings. Parking lots should not occupy more than roughly 1/3 of the frontage, or no more than 75 feet, of a

pedestrian-oriented street, such as retail "Main Streets" and local streets. Other streets may not be able to maintain this criterion.

Structured and below-grade parking is strongly encouraged on Redevelopable and Infill Sites in conjunction with new development or as part of a comprehensive reuse plan; it is encouraged, but not required, in New Growth Areas. Underground parking is preferred over above-ground structure parking. If structured parking is not immediately economically viable, development plans should indicate how structured parking and more intensive uses could be integrated into the site at a later date.

Size of Surface Parking Lots

Large surface parking lots should be visually and functionally segmented into several smaller lots. The size of any single surface parking lot should be limited to three acres, unless divided by a street or building.

Too often, the front facades of new shopping and office complexes are dominated by large surface parking lots. These expanses of asphalt are hostile to pedestrians and are disincentives to walking. To make this type of parking lot more human-scale, they should be seg-mented into smaller units by placing a street through two parking areas or locating a building between parking areas. If a single use will require a surface parking lot in excess of three acres, structured parking should be strongly encouraged.

Surface Parking Redevelopment

Land devoted to surface parking lots should be reduced through redevelopment and construction of structured parking facilities. The layout and configuration of surface parking lots should accommodate future redevelopment; design studies showing placement of future buildings and parking structures should be provided.

EXISTING SURFACE PARKING LOT

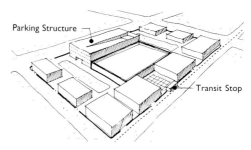

FUTURE INTENSIFICATION

Opportunities for redeveloping existing surface parking lots with buildings and structured parking should be strongly pursued in order to more efficiently utilize land near transit stops.

Additionally, in early phases of development, when land values are still relatively low, some sites may be developed with surface parking lots. Potential redevelopment of surface parking should be considered when the project is designed, and should be strongly encouraged to redevelop with more intensive uses as the area matures.

Land in the vicinity of the transit stop should be developed with the greatest intensity in order to provide the most opportunities for transit ridership. As land values increase, redevelopment of surface parking lots to more intensive uses will augment this desired density.

Retail in Structured Parking Lots

Parking structures should not be allowed to dominate the street frontage. Retail uses should be encouraged on the first floor of street-side edges of parking structures.

Like surface parking lots, parking structures that line streets do not provide interest, safety, or shelter for the pedestrian. Retail uses should be located on the ground floor of parking garages and incorporated into the building's design. Office buildings can also be designed so that the active use portions of the building face the street and wrap around an interior parking structure rather than sit on top of a podium of parking. Minor portions of parking structures that do not have first-level retail uses must be articulated and otherwise have an appearance similar to the buildings they serve.

PREFERRED

DISCOURAGED

Parking Lot Landscaping

All parking lots should be planted with sufficient trees so that within ten years 70 percent of the surface area of the lot is shaded. Additionally, parking lots should be screened from streets by non-bermed landscape treatments. Where possible, overflow parking areas should be developed with a permeable surface.

This guideline is intended to achieve an environment that is comfortable to pedestrians. Trees should be located along walkways; perimeter landscaping should screen views of cars, but not block views of retail facades. Tree canopies should be trimmed to provide shade, but should allow building visibility. Asphalt area can be limited by converting the peak parking areas to permeable surfaces such as gravel. This will allow water to percolate into the water table and will

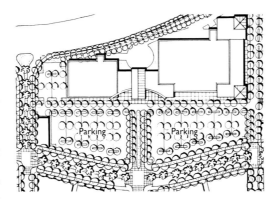

visually limit the "sea of asphalt" atmosphere many major shopping areas develop.

Trees and other landscaping are particularly important for surface parking lots which absorb significant amounts of solar heat and create uncomfortable places for pedestrians. Landscaping along parking lot perimeters should also be provided to soften the visual impact of rows of parked cars and define the edge of the sidewalk.

The projects in this section represent applications of the guidelines in a variety of conditions. Each project is, in some way, an expression of the fundamental principles of design articulated in the guidelines, each in a different location, market, and political atmosphere. They span from regional plans to small infill projects, from urban sites to suburban new towns. Their range is meant to demonstrate the diversity of this approach to growth. In all cases, the projects are pedestrian-friendly, diverse in use and population, and have a clear public focus. Yet they are grounded in reality – operating in the current marketplace and standing the tests of client needs, public input, technical feasibility, and financial viability.

Most of the projects illustrated here were developed using a community workshop process. This process varied with each situation but always had the common goal of involving citizens in the design process. We view the workshop process as an important means to several ends. First, the public should to be informed about the real range of options. Too often, neighbors assume development has to have the negative characteristics of sprawl, more traffic, more asphalt, and more environmental blight. Our first workshop typically presents and describes different types of development, including mixed-use neighborhoods. Second, community input is irreplaceable from a designer's point of view. No matter how many studies one does, the locals always know more about the nature and history of their place than any professional. An early workshop gathers information from the locals in the form of facts, goals, and concepts. Asking people to use these categories often clarifies the information. Third, neighbors need to be part of the design process. They need to understand the trade-offs of site-specific planning and the scale of what is possible, and be involved in the dynamics of working in a team. Typically, we devote one workshop to citizens working in small groups to select, annotate, redesign, or add to plans which are basically feasible. Finally, neighbors should see and understand the results.

This section is organized into four parts: Regional Plans, Station Area Plans, New Neighborhoods, and Towns and New Towns. Regional Plans demonstrate the overall framework for growth in a metropolis (and contain, in some cases, the sites for smaller projects). Station Area Plans are typically for sites developed at higher and more urban densities, generally located on a fixed-rail line, and are defined in the guidelines as Urban TODs. These Urban TODs can represent infill and redevelopment or they can occur in suburban areas at major transit stations. New Neighborhoods, called Neighborhood TODs in the guidelines, are lower density, contain less commercial development, and are generally found in suburban areas, either as infill or as new growth. Towns and New Towns are either part of a larger metropolitan region or completely independent; they can involve the infill or redevelopment of existing small towns or the development of entirely new communities.

Regional Plans

The Regional Plans resemble the urban patterns generated when trolleys dominated our cities and streetcar suburbs developed at the periphery. But this pattern is not simply a return to the past; it is the consequence of contemporary forces. The fundamental fact is that growth is now *nodal* and decentralizing at a rapid rate. Many of the urban components not present forty years ago are preeminent now: regional shopping, decentralized employment centers, large-scale production housing, and environmental constraints, to name a few. This trend of retail, transit, and business toward identifiable nodes, rather than strips or urban centers, directs the form and location of the development in these plans. This nodal pattern projects the next generation of growth around transit and at urban sub-centers as well as in the traditional central business district.

The Portland project is a good example of this nodal pattern. The small town of Beaverton became an urban sub-center, providing an employment destination closer than downtown Portland for the new development of Washington County. This is not unlike the development of Silicon Valley in relationship to San Francisco, where a group of suburban small towns evolved into a major employment center under the decentralizing force of modern business. Although there is little difference here in the regional distribution of development or the essential fact of economic decentralization, there is a big difference in the type of the development – a necklace of integrated neighborhoods connected by transit, rather than isolated land uses along a freeway.

Two of the Regional Plans, Portland and Sacramento, were developed for large, fast-growing suburban counties and therefore did not include their central city areas. Consequently, these projects over emphasize the suburban dimension of growth. The work does not intentionally exclude urban infill from the regional program for growth, but the scope of each project does tend to create an incomplete picture. In each case an Urban Growth Boundary (UGB) is the handmaid of the transit-based growth. The UGB is central to the strategy of containing growth and directing it to support transit and infill. Since these studies do not include the central city, they cannot fully address the larger issues of distribution of growth and a complete transit system. In contrast, the City of San Diego is so large that it becomes a region unto itself, complete with city center, suburbs, and undeveloped surrounding lands. Its plan offers a more complete vision of regional planning.

Merced is a small city coping with the growth caused by flight from the Bay Area. Its plan clearly shows the progression of settlement patterns, from classic small-town grid, through suburban cul-de-sac, to the new plan for mixed-use nodes. Unlike the complex jurisdictional mix of the larger metropolitan regions, this stand-alone city is largely free of the contradictions and limitations that adjacent cities and towns can create. Short of policies by its surrounding county and the overall economic forces at the state level, it can control its own destiny.

All of the Regional Plans are designed to cope with large growth pressures. They do not address conditions more typical of current East Coast regions – slower growth rates in more built-out suburbs and towns. Because of the high rate of growth in the western cities, the emphasis of the illustrated plans is on large-scale new growth areas or major infill opportunities. A much smaller, fine-grain infill opportunity exists in all these areas but is overshadowed by the sheer magnitude of growth. This smaller infill opportunity can follow the same principles as larger growth areas but in more site-specific and idiosyncratic ways. Many eastern regions would require this finer scale of intervention. Such stable areas have the advantage of focusing on this dimension of growth.

Station Area Plans and New Neighborhoods

The Station Area Plans vary in location, but share the common feature of a fixed-rail transit stop. Their sites range from inner-city locations such as Brooklyn and downtown Sacramento to suburban rail stops such as Mission Valley in San Diego and the Jackson-Taylor neighborhood in San Jose. The residential side of these projects is consistently high density, ranging from a low of 15 units per acre up to 70. The commercial uses vary considerably, with the Brooklyn and Sacramento sites affording large quantities of office development and the others a mix of retail and employment. This centralized office development at station areas can help the economic revitalization of the inner city while supporting transit. Ironically, the San Diego site incorporates a major discount retailer of approximately 120,000 sq-ft – a distinctly un-pedestrian scale and use. This demonstrates that the design principles are flexible enough to include these particularly modern trends in retailing. All the projects share the guidelines' features of central public spaces and parks, a diverse mix of uses, and a strong orientation to the street.

The Colma project demonstrates a key danger of specialists planning in a vacuum. The engineers for BART, the heavy-rail system in the Bay Area, designed the station for the uses they controlled: a park-and-ride lot and a major bus drop-off area. The result, sadly, is a station isolated from the neighborhood by noisy buses on one side and a six-story parking structure on the other. If a larger vision for the development of the neighborhood had been coordinated with their planning, the bus area could have been incorporated into the parking structure – and one side of the station could have greeted the pedestrian. Unfortunately, such integrated planning is rare and, even worse, our new transit systems are being designed as if park-and-ride was the only meaningful form of access. Transit agencies should plan for TOD-like development around their station facilities to avoid precluding the possibility of such mixed-use neighborhoods.

The New Neighborhoods are perhaps the most interesting of the planning types. They represent the straightforward transformation of the suburban landscape. In fact one, Laguna West, is a reconfiguration of a standard piece of suburban sprawl. The redesign maintains the density, mix and building types originally programmed for standard development, but changes the relationships between uses, the street configurations, the orientation of the buildings to streets, and the layout of the parks and public elements. This is perhaps the most important test of the concepts presented here. Without changing the currently immutable marketplace criteria for housing, retail, and parking, significant improvements in travel behavior and the sense of community were achieved through design. Of course, some of the commonly held development rules were modi-

fied, such as garage placement and street widths. But the real transformation was established through a new set of relationships among the given uses. The other examples in this section are variations on this theme – establishing a pedestrian scale through a reordering of elements such as streets, parks, public buildings, and retail centers without radically changing the fundamental program of development.

There are several formal tendencies shown here which may seem idiosyncratic. The radial street pattern is one. The use of this pattern is the result of three ideas. First and most simply, a diagonal is the shortest distance between two points and that is important to the person on foot. A single-point local destination is implicit in every plan because retail and transit, the prime uses at the core, are essentially nodal and do not function well in a linear form. Second, radial streets add a powerful contrast to local streets, distinguishing "civic" roads from neighborhood streets and adding a certain grandeur rarely found in the suburbs. And third, radials add focus and clarity to the identity of the center. They are a special version of what we have come to call "connector" streets which replace the ubiquitous "collector" streets of suburbia and do not direct all traffic to the arterials. The "connector" streets are more frequent than collectors and lead to the center of the neighborhood before accessing the arterial.

Each of the plans creates a mixed-use center around a village green – perhaps another design idiosyncrasy. This approach allows the different uses to support one another through their interaction and proximity. The village green is a design device which serves many ends. Employment provides shoppers for the retail and riders for the transit system; retail provides local destinations for workers, residents, and transit riders; and the village green provides a meeting ground for all. In some cases stores front onto the green. This allows more visibility and front door parking than a "Main Street" retail configuration. If a residential or office use is added above, these users benefit from views of the green. Some of the more important civic uses, such as the town hall in Laguna West or daycare in Dupont Landing, can be placed in the green. The green, therefore, becomes the literal and symbolic center of the town, the physical and visual meeting ground of people as well as land uses.

Towns and New Towns

Finding a conclusive definition for a "Town" is troublesome at best. There is no simple criteria of size, separation, or focus possible today. A town's size can vary dramatically, as can its density or focus. Ebenezer Howard set his Garden Cities at a population of around 30,000. A high school needs a population of 20,000, a community college 60,000, and regional shopping a market area of 100,000. Many of the best university towns are around 50,000, but this is a meaningless number because they typically exist in a larger metropolitan area. Many towns are now consumed by their regions and have lost much of their traditional autonomy. While they rarely have urban densities, their mix and intensity can vary greatly. They traditionally can have many different focuses and identities formed by the dominance of a specific commercial use, industrial base, one company or product, tourism, or education.

I use several criteria to distinguish Towns from suburban New Growth Areas. Towns are larger in physical size than one pedestrian neighborhood, and they have a substantial employment base with a regional commercial or civic focus. The New Towns presented here all share the common trait of having been conceived partly to siphon growth from the surrounding area, thereby protecting the quality and physical separation between existing towns. Included is one example of how an existing small town, Loomis, chose to grow internally without giving up its scale and character. Like inner-city infill, this is an important model of how the guidelines apply to developed areas as well as greenfields.

The large New Towns – Placer Villages and Lexington Park – have several interesting qualities which may separate them from the New Town experiments of the 1960s. First they are multi-nodal. Each village within the New Town is scaled to the pedestrian and is in effect a microcosm of the whole. This structure can allow the towns to grow in coherent phases, both economically and socially. Each village would have a different focus so that latter phase villages could develop the cultural, regional shopping, or employment uses needed by larger populations. The early-phase villages would be primarily residential with complementary retail, civic activities, and services proportioned to their needs.

The second quality that differentiates these New Towns from their counterparts of the sixties and seventies is the current economic environment. Earlier, the local and state tax base was healthier and could provide a base for affordable development within existing jurisdictions – the Columbias and Restons did not have a great economic advantage. After the tax revolts of the 1980s, property tax limits, along with the state fiscal crisis, have redirected the costs of many basic services from general fund tax base to developer fees. As a result, the newcomer, more often than not, pays more than his share. In this context, the sum of high land costs and these demanding fees often means that affordable housing is rare within existing municipalities. New Towns, through efficient infrastructure and lower basic land costs, can become a prime means of providing the entry-level housing a region needs to maintain a healthy employment base. Placer Villages is a good example of this arithmetic.

•   •   •

It is important to remember that no project shown here is hypothetical. Each had a real client, whether public or private, a specific site, concerned and sometimes angry neighbors, strict financing formulas, outdated codes, and sometimes demanding deadlines. They are, therefore, examples of what is possible today, from an economic, market, political, technical, institutional, and environmental standpoint. Some did not succeed, some are still in process, and some are under construction. But given the constraints of the world today these projects demonstrate some of what is possible. In times to come much more, I hope, will become possible.

REGIONAL PLANS

STATION AREA PLANS

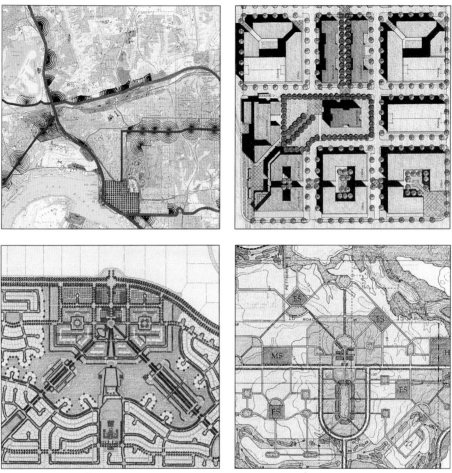

NEW NEIGHBORHOODS

TOWNS AND NEW TOWNS

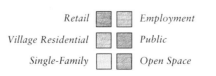

Retail

Employment

Village Residential

Public

Single-Family

Open Space

LUTRAQ
Making the Land Use, Transportation,
Air Quality Connection
Portland, Oregon

LUTRAQ is a national demonstration project sponsored by 1000 Friends of Oregon, a nationally renowned environmental group that helped create Oregon's state-legislated regional plans and Urban Growth Boundaries. To counter a proposed $200 million beltway around the west side of Portland that would violate the Urban Growth Boundary, they have supported a study of alternative land use and transit options to demonstrate that more freeways are not the only solution to increasing traffic. Transit-Oriented Development (TOD) patterns were used to show that land use can effectively reduce auto dependence, increase mobility, minimize air quality impacts, and create more affordable communities.

The LUTRAQ land use plan reallocates a projected population growth of 160,000 in Washington County from standard sprawl into a mixed-use pattern that supports the planned light rail and bus network extensions. The plan simply rearranged the land uses which

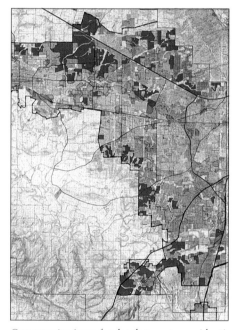

Opportunity Areas for development were identified by combining areas within reach of transit with those that had no environmental constraints or viable existing uses. The red areas represent new growth opportunities and the yellow areas have redevelopment potential.

Environmental factors along with existing development helped define the potential growth areas. These open space elements included creeks and streams, flood plains, ridge lands, sensitive habitat, and wetlands.

The alternative land use map for the west side of Portland shows four principle land use types. Mixed-Use Centers are shown in a bold grid, Urban TODs with heavy circles, Neighborhood TODs with light circles, and Secondary Areas with dots. Over 75 percent of all new housing in this proposal would be within one-half mile of transit and configured in a walkable mixed-use community.

were predicted to develop in the next twenty years; the overall density and proportion of different housing types were not altered. Four new types of development were planned: Mixed-Use Centers to urbanize existing downtown areas through redevelopment and infill; Urban TODs at station areas along the planned light rail lines; Neighborhood TODs within a short feeder bus ride of the light rail; and Secondary Areas within a mile of each center. The Mixed-Use Centers and Urban TODs both had an average 15 housing units per acre with high ratios of employment. The Neighborhood TODs had 8 units per acre average and an emphasis on resident-serving commercial. Standard single-family densities were placed in Secondary Areas.

The most interesting aspect of the study has been the enhancement of the standard traffic prediction computer model. To date, the traffic models have not incorporated the potential benefits of walkable neighborhoods and mixed-use areas, they – in what could be called a self-fulfilling prophecy – only project current travel behavior into the future. The model was enhanced with a "Pedestrian Friendliness" factor and a "Heterogeneity" factor to simulate the impact of neighborhoods that were walkable, had convenient local destinations, and accessible transit. The computer model results show a four fold increase in walking and two and one-half times more transit use.

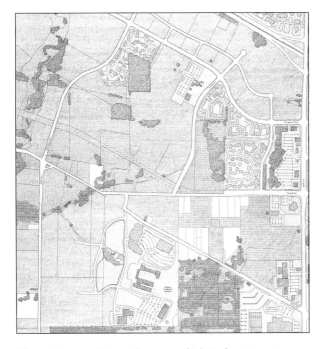

The existing conditions of an area which is about to experience rapid growth in the western part of the Portland region. Note the apartments and shopping center on the upper right. People who live there cannot walk conveniently to the shops because the retail area is walled-off in the rear and bounded by major roads on the other three sides. In the upper left is a creek and in the lower right is a forest which will be preserved.

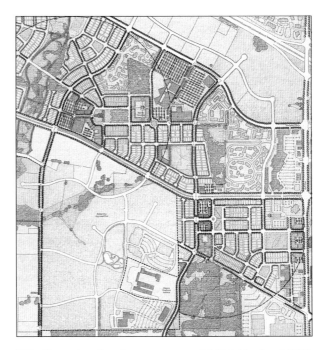

This illustrative plan shows two potential Neighborhood TOD centers, each with a retail and civic focus, a local connecting street network, and a variety of housing types. The large industrial and commercial uses shown are unfortunately fixed because of recent project commitments. Each neighborhood is bounded by a 2,000 foot walking distance or a major arterial roadway. A feeder bus would stop at each center and run to the light rail station one and one-half miles away.

The existing conditions around a planned light rail station show the standard sprawl patterns typical in this area. Fortunately, several of the subdivisions have roads stubbing out into undeveloped parcels that can allow local street connections to the potential neighborhood center and transit stop. The land south of the tracks and to the east of the collector road is currently zoned for office, a use which is appropriate for a major transit station.

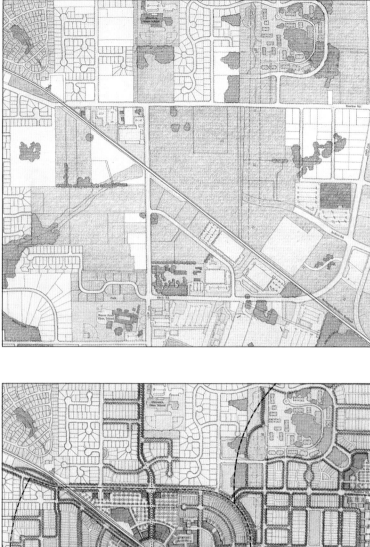

This is an example of the type of development which is proposed for a light rail station area. At the station is a village green surrounded by a retail center, cinema, daycare, apartments, and offices. Radial streets connect to neighborhoods of townhouse, small-lot single-family, and traditional single-family lots. Neighborhood parks are within two blocks of each house and an existing elementary school is located at the southern edge of the site. At the upper right is a Neighborhood TOD which is separated from the station area by a six-lane arterial, but will be connected by a feeder bus.

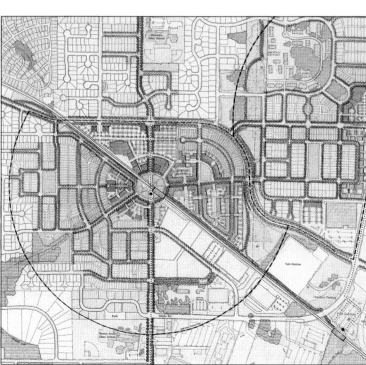

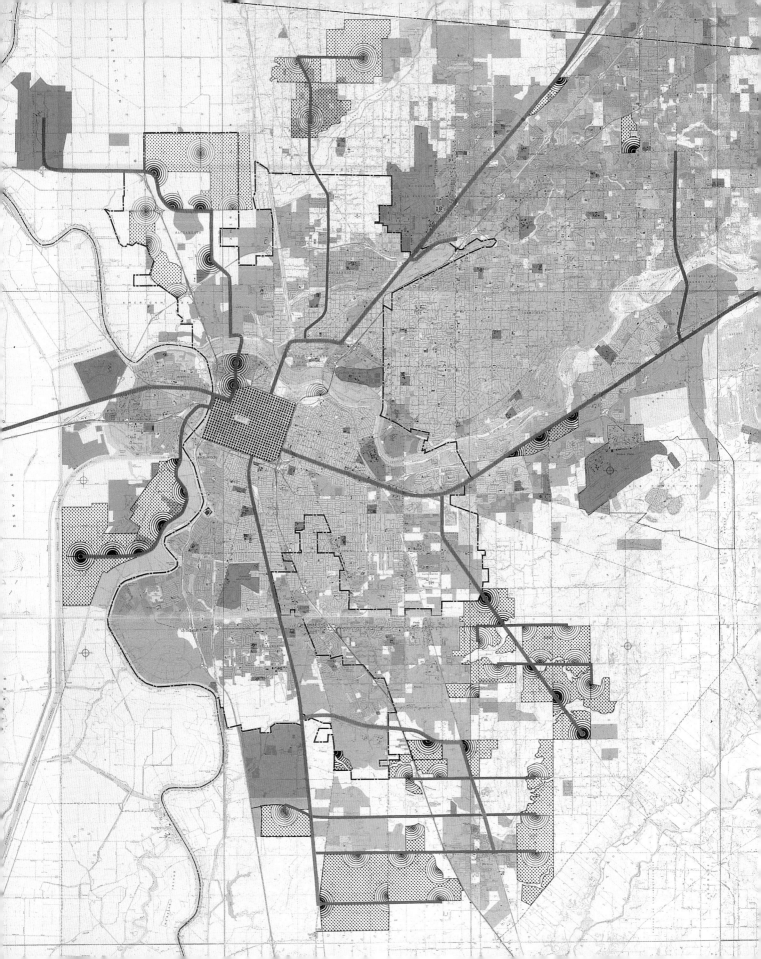

Sacramento County General Plan Update
and Southport Area Plan
Sacramento, California

Sacramento County is using Transit-Oriented Development Guidelines as a mechanism to implement their updated General Plan. With a projected growth of 270,000 in the next twenty years, Sacramento County is dominated by low density patterns of development and is quickly approaching the crisis of many suburban regions: traffic congestion, loss of open space, loss of affordable housing, and poor air quality. Faced with the clear limits of "more of the same" and a progressive environmental community which advocated an alternate to sprawl, the County's planners developed a plan based on a new Transit-Oriented Development pattern. A set of TOD Design Guidelines were developed to augment the single-use zoning ordinances of the previous General Plan.

The new General Plan uses the region's expanding light rail system to locate major New Growth Areas (see Laguna West and Calvine Specific Area Plan), as well as identify infill and redevelopment sites (see Capital River Park). Each New Growth Area will have a series of Urban and Neighborhood TODs with Secondary Areas. In addition to the designated growth areas, the plan creates an "Urban Service Boundary" which identifies the ultimate limit of development for the county and preserves the Sacramento and Consumes River corridors, along with prime agriculture lands to the south.

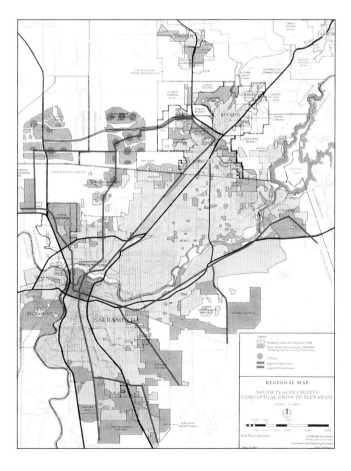

(Left) This illustration of the Sacramento Metropolitan Area shows "New Growth Areas" largely in the southern parts of the county and in West Sacramento, along with a significant redevelopment area in the old rail yards of the central city. Each growth area is in a planned transit corridor and is zoned for a mix of Urban (heavy circles) and Neighborhood (light circles) TODs. The area across the river just to the south of the city center is the Southport site, illustrated on the following pages.

A Regional Growth Plan for the Sacramento area covers five counties and seven towns. This map diagrams a growth alternative which expands Sacramento County's New Growth Areas with two satellite New Towns in the north, along with the Southport area in West Sacramento. Each is within transit distance of the downtown and each brings with it a greenbelt which would help secure a regional growth boundary. The light brown represents existing developed areas and the dark brown shows the quantity of development projected for the next twenty years.

Unfortunately, there is no regional entity which can coordinate and enforce the growth boundary in the adjoining counties. The problem for the Sacramento County plan is that these adjacent jurisdictions may become havens for sprawl, as piecemeal growth seeks to avoid the County's mixed-use requirements and the Urban Service Boundary.

The politics of such a plan are complex and involve a diverse group of special interests: land owners, developers, environmentalists, local neighborhood groups, various public agencies, builders, and the Chamber of Commerce, to name a few. Many of these groups were fearful of change and its ambiguous effects. High on the list of concerns were the market viability of mixed-use suburbs, the fear that TODs were a Trojan horse of apartment ghettos, and potential changes in the average residential densities county-wide. Added to these concerns were the normal politics of development: where should growth be located, how much development should be planned for, and whether there should be an ultimate edge to the region at all.

The plan below is for the Southport area of West Sacramento. It is an example of the type of development which the County plan calls for in its designated growth areas.

This plan for a 40,000 population increase in the Southport area of West Sacramento was a design competition. The development in the middle of the central axial road existed and the industrial lands along the deep water channel were fixed. Our plan called for six villages on a new light rail line from downtown Sacramento along an open space river edge. Each village would have a different character: several fronting the open space, one with a marina, one near a golf course, and one at the bridge entry.

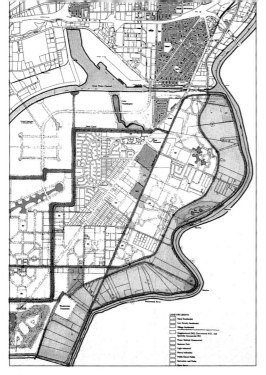

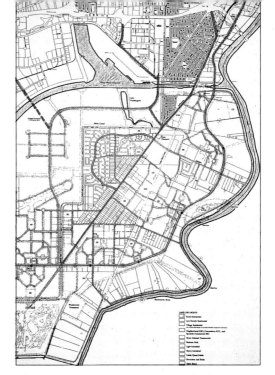

The open space diagram for Southport shows a major greenbelt along the river. This area is not only prime agricultural land, but a rare habitat for the endangered Swainson's Hawk. The plan envisions a series of villages looking out over the open space to the river.

The circulation diagram shows a network of local "connector" streets which reduce the need for major arterials in the area. This capillary system of roads allows local trips to avoid the major through streets, thereby reducing the size of such facilities. This reduced demand amounted to approximately $40 million in construction savings when compared to a standard arterial system – equivalent to cost of the proposed light rail system in this area.

An illustrative plan of one of the villages shows the center with transit stop facing the open space and river. A person living in this village would be 5 miles from downtown Sacramento by light rail and would have the convenience of pedestrian access to local shops, elementary school, and neighborhood parks. As in the European countryside, the village would be a stones throw from open space.

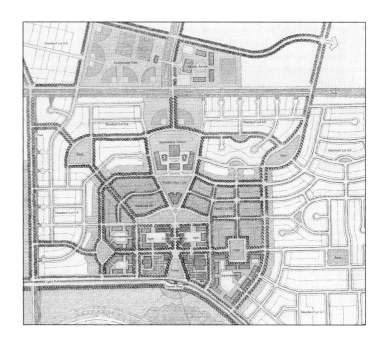

San Diego Design Guidelines
San Diego, California

The City of San Diego, one of the fastest growing urban areas in California, has adopted Transit-Oriented Development Design Guidelines as a key component in their Land Guidance and Urban Form programs. TODs are being used to help the city reduce urban sprawl, plan the urbanized area efficiently, encourage infill and redevelopment, and support the trolley and bus transit system. A particular focus of the guidelines is encouraging infill and redevelopment in existing neighborhoods. In addition to providing design guidelines for site selection, development patterns, and transit integration, the work includes an Implementation Strategy that outlines the steps necessary to fully adopt the principles and specific recommendations of the design guidelines into city-wide zoning, street standards, and other policies.

The process of preparation and adoption of the guidelines was inclusive and very effective. A 40 person steering committee, including a broad range of public and private interests, set the overall direction and then reviewed each guideline individually, giving input and suggesting modifications. The draft guidelines were then tested on three sites by a workshop of citizens, professionals, and City staff. They used the guidelines to design the future development and redevelopment of an existing suburban station area, an industrial zone, and a shopping mall. Finally, City staff presented the ideas, guidelines, and illustrative designs to every neighborhood group and community planning board within the city. This exhaustive input and education process proved successful in both tailoring the guidelines to the unique qualities of San Diego and allowing people to understand the changes that were proposed.

The map to the left illustrates part of the transit area development potential of San Diego's 330 square miles, one of the largest cities in the country in land area. It shows the development and redevelopment sites in the immediate vicinity of the Central Business District, some on existing and planned extensions of the trolley, some on express bus routes. The next extension of the trolley line runs through Mission Valley along the San Diego River – the first TODs site on this new trolley line is illustrated in the Tecolote plan on the following page and the fifth to the east is the Rio Vista West site, a project shown later.

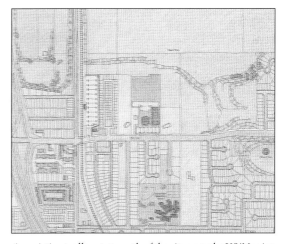

An existing trolley stop south of the city near the US/Mexico border. Note that the stop is surrounded by parking and even residents of the adjacent trailer park have to walk out onto the major arterial and back through the parking lot to get to the station. The lands to the north are designated for regional open space.

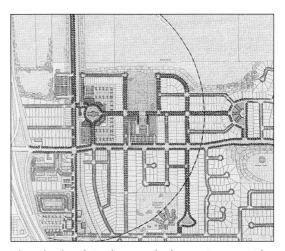

The redeveloped site shows a suburban station area with a green, small shops, and a reconfiguration of the trailer park. A new local street network provides direct pedestrian connections to the station north of the major east-west arterial and four local street crossings to the south. The park-and-ride lot is relocated to the west of the tracks.

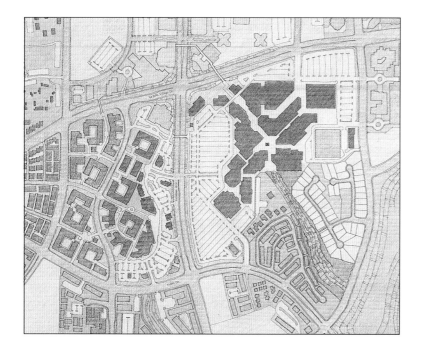

The University City area of San Diego was planned in the seventies and built over the last twenty years. It is mixed-use and fairly dense, but has no pedestrian quality. This map of an existing area shows how apartments, a major shopping center, hotel, and offices can add up to congestion rather than community. Each land use connects to the six-lane arterial system rather than to one another. Several unused pedestrian bridges fruitlessly span the arterials, connecting one parking lot with another.

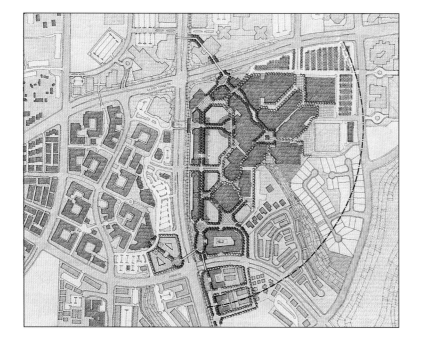

This site represents one of the most interesting opportunities the suburbs have to offer: conversion of commercial parking lots into mixed-use developments with parking structures. In this case a regional shopping center's parking lot is infilled with a "Main Street" which has housing over shops on one side and shops on the ground floor of parking structures on the other. This Main Street leads to a new trolley stop at one end and a residential development with a pedestrian bridge and mini-park at the other.

The Tecolote District is a typical older industrial area with many uses which are economically marginal. The area is severely impacted by high traffic volumes and the adjacent freeway. A major influence not show on this map of existing development is the University of California at San Diego, located uphill to the northeast, which would draw students to the new trolley station.

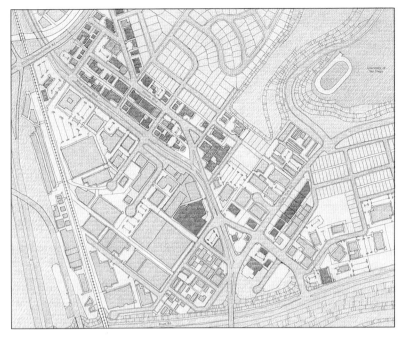

With the addition of a new trolley station directly connecting to the downtown, this industrial area could experience an economic and land use transformation. This illustrative plan shows some of the industrial areas converting to live-work lofts, as has happened in special areas of other cities. In order to eliminate a pedestrian barrier, the major arterial is divided into a one-way couplet – each side lined with lanes for convenience parking. A green surrounded by retail is added at the station and the lands nearest the University are zoned for housing.

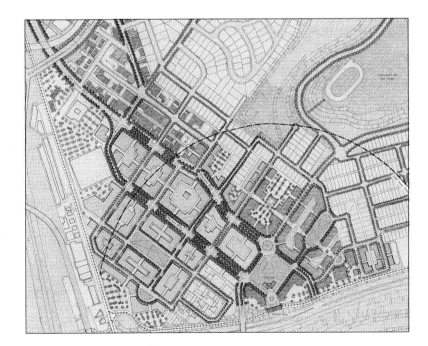

Merced Villages
Merced, California

Merced, population 56,000, is a fast-growing town in the Central Valley of California. Once primarily an agricultural economy, it has recently been inundated with Bay Area escapees looking for affordable housing and a comprehensible community. The overall master plan for the existing and planned sections of the city reveals an interesting progression. Starting with the traditional grid-iron town centered on the railway station, the area immediately to the north exploded with suburban growth in the seventies and eighties. This area, featuring cul-de-sacs and an agglomeration of retail uses, ironically has a lower density than the original mixed-use town, but has the worst traffic congestion in the city. The next

generation of growth would have a completely different form, combining the mixed-use characteristics of the original town with the nodal quality of walkable neighborhoods.

This plan is unusual in that it accommodates a forty year growth demand, rather than the typical twenty year planning period. The City had developed the concept of three new villages to accommodate 75,000 of new population and had laid out a street network which included three expressway status roads and freeway-type interchanges. The redesign of this "three village plan" substituted nine pedestrian villages within an arterial grid – approximately one neighborhood in each 640

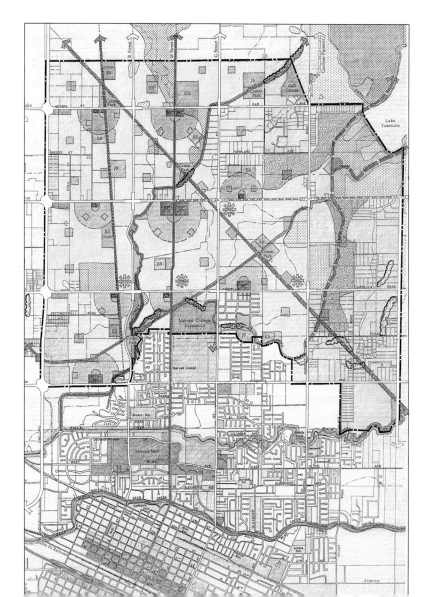

acre section. This configuration, which reduced traffic demand on the arterials, resulted in a circulation system of four-lane streets with surface intersections – a major reduction in infrastructure costs.

A detailed economic analysis rendered a specific program for the amount and type of retail which would be required by the growth area. This retail component was distributed between the nine villages helping to create variety in each. Through the center of the site a new trolley system would be constructed, making those villages on the transit line major community centers. Along with the land use map, the City adopted a companion set of Design Guidelines to direct mixed-use development.

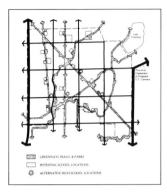

The open space diagram shows a series of schools, neighborhood parks, and larger community parks linked by a set of "greenways" which follow creeks and open space easements, and include pedestrian and bicycle trails. Where these trails cross an arterial an underpass will be constructed.

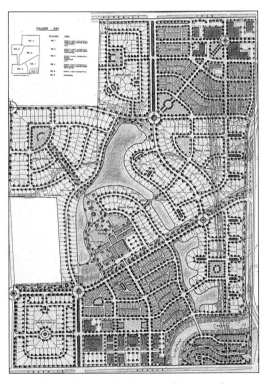

Two of the villages within the overall master plan were designed for a property owner in the southwestern corner of the growth area. Called North Park Villages, the plan shows two retail centers each with a village green and moderate density housing. In the middle a lake, elementary school, and community recreation facility are shared by both villages and the single-family neighborhoods.

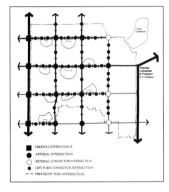

The circulation diagram shows the primary arterial grid on one mile centers along with the types of intersections and proposed spacing for each crossing. A set of "connector" streets (not shown) would subdivide the interior of each section, allowing convenient local trips by foot, bike, or car to take place without the use of the arterials.

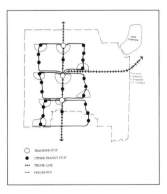

The transit diagram shows the "M Street Transitway" at the center, with three feeder bus loops which would have stops in the outer villages. The transitway would provide direct service to the center of town, to the inter-city rail station, and to a potential site for one of the next generation of University of California campuses.

Atlantic Center

Brooklyn, New York

This master plan represents an often frustrated attempt to direct growth into prime inner-city areas that are well-served by transit, rather than allowing the jobs, housing and activity to be dissipated into the suburbs. Sadly in this case, the project was delayed in court by a well-meaning but myopic environmental group, resulting in the demise of the plan. Questioned on its local air quality impacts, the transit-oriented plan was never compared to the impacts of spreading a similar quantity of development across New Jersey in subdivisions and office parks. Meant as a key component in the general revitalization of downtown Brooklyn, this mixed-use development would have placed 688 units of "affordable housing" and 2.7 million square feet of back office space on 12 acres at one of the region's largest transit

stations, Atlantic Terminal of the Long Island Railroad.

The master plan organizes four-story Brownstone courtyard apartment buildings around a crescent park and along streets which reestablish the lost fabric of a neighborhood decimated by 1960s redevelopment. Office buildings along Atlantic Avenue would shield the residential neighborhood from the adjacent train tracks. Daycare and community centers were situated at the base of the crescent park. Neighborhood grocery stores and small retail stores line the neighborhood's edge, while larger retail facilities were planned near the underground terminal. Two large office towers would have housed the majority of the back office space at the northwest end of the site near the famous Williamsburg Bank Building.

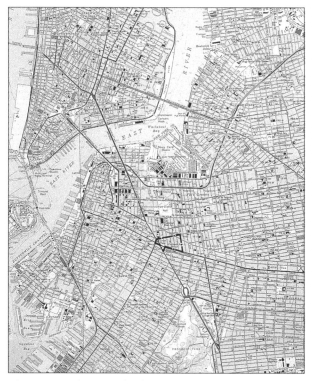

The site is in an historic redevelopment area, between older Brownstone neighborhoods and 1960s-style co-op apartments. Atlantic and Flatbush Avenues are major arterials which border two sides of the site.

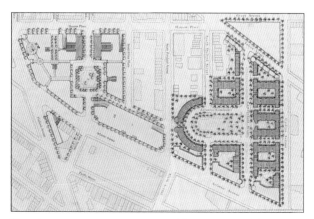

The plan creates two centers, one with a commercial focus over Atlantic Terminal and the other a residential neighborhood wrapping around a crescent-shaped park. Between is a multi-purpose building with a major grocery store. The commercial area includes a skylight concourse entry to the station with shopping, entertainment, and restaurants. Two major office building towers centered on an urban park sit adjacent to the terminal and concourse. The residential area features small shops, daycare, the park, and nine courtyards.

The view along Atlantic and Flatbush shows the low-rise "back office" buildings with ground floor retail. The famous Williamsburg Bank building beyond is complemented by one of the two new towers. In order to attract businesses which would have moved to the suburbs, these new towers must have large floors which contribute to their bulk.

Jackson-Taylor Revitalization Strategy
San Jose, California

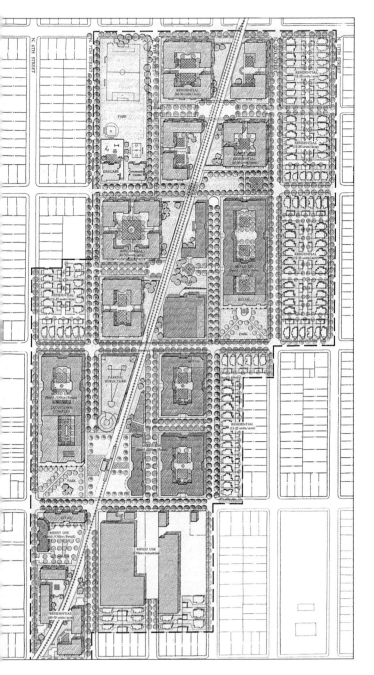

This project represents an ubiquitous urban opportunity – to transform old rail-oriented industrial zones into mixed-use neighborhoods with excellent transit service. In this case an underutilized freight train right-of-way would be converted to an extension for BART, the regional commuter rail service, and the adjacent decaying industrial sites would redevelop adding density and diversity to a semi-suburban section of town. Much of San Jose is marked by an odd combination of an urban street system and a low-rise, low-density building fabric. Known as a "suburban city," San Jose has done much to urbanize its downtown through intelligent planning, redevelopment, and a new light rail system. This project would extend this largely successful effort by beginning to create a series of urban nodes radiating from the central city.

The plan provides for the gradual transition of a 75 acre area directly north of downtown from low intensity industrial and residential uses to a mix of retail, office, and medium and high density housing. Originally the site of San Jose's fruit and vegetable canneries, this Revitalization Strategy takes advantage of its prox-

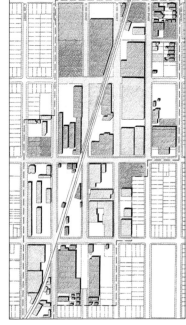

The various colors represent the economic viability of the existing industrial uses on the site, and their potential to redevelop over time. Purple represents parcels expected to redevelop immediately; lavender parcels may change in three to five years; and grey parcels are expected to remain for a longer period.

imity to existing light rail and a proposed on-site BART station to increase housing, neighborhood shopping, and job opportunities. Weaving together two diverse ethnic neighborhoods, several unique development opportunities are provided, such as a Japanese business/cultural center and a local "mercado" for the Hispanic community.

The plan establishes a network of neighborhood parks, plazas, daycare, and community centers connected by comfortable, landscaped, pedestrian-oriented streets. The proposed residential buildings at the site's edge maintain the rhythm and character of the surrounding single-family neighborhood and provide a sympathetic interface with the surrounding residences. Within this framework, up to 2,100 residential units and over 800,000 square feet of retail, office, and industrial uses are allowed. The plan was prepared for the City of San Jose and included extensive input from neighborhood groups, property owners, and concerned citizens. It is a good example of the TOD concept applied to the redevelopment and revitalization of an underutilized inner-city neighborhood.

The rail right-of-way through the site would close the loop of BART on both sides of the San Francisco Bay. The San Jose light rail system is shown crossing this right-of-way and running into the center of the city.

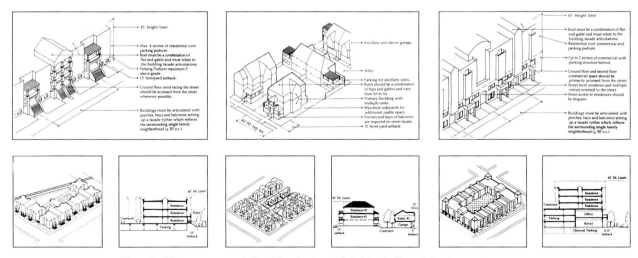

Three building types were defined for the site with height, bulk, and density requirements. Each of these types has design guidelines to maintain the urban quality of the neighborhood. The building types range from three unit parcels at the edge (15 units per acre), to podium apartments (50 units per acre) and mixed-use buildings on the site's interior.

139

Colma BART Specific Area Plan
Daly City, California

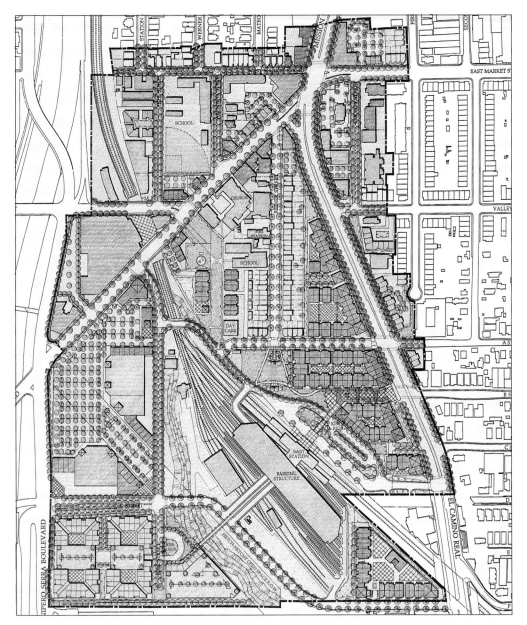

The BART station is located over a train maintenance yard that is effectively a channel separating the site into two. The section between the freeway and station area will be dedicated to large-scale retail and office uses. A passenger drop-off area at the foot of the pedestrian bridge west of the station is lined with convenience shops.

On the other side of the station, the plan integrates high density housing into the scale of the existing neighborhood. The street grid is extended from across the arterial and the internal streets are redeveloped with trees and sidewalks. A drop-off area on the arterial is connected to the station by a grand public stairway.

This project highlights the challenge of coordinating many jurisdictions and property owners in an effort to develop an appropriate level of intensity at what will be a prime transit stop. Two transit agencies, two Cities, a County, and a variety of neighborhood groups were involved in a community planning process which had to reverse previous piecemeal planning, along with many misconceptions about the impacts of transit. An example of negative "special interest group" planning was the BART engineers' plan for the station itself. Prior to any land use planning around the station, BART finalized a flawed and too often repeated station design: a six-story parking structure on one side and four lanes of bus stalls on the other, completely cutting off the surrounding area. In the engineer's eye the station is seen as a transfer point only, not as the potential center of a neighborhood or a pedestrian destination.

The intent of the new Colma BART Specific Area Plan is urban "place-making" in what is now a semi-suburban area. The first new BART station to be built in 25 years, the plan for the surrounding area of 110 acres demonstrates how a large region-serving transportation facility can be integrated into a local urban fabric, used to generate new commercial activity, and focus housing demand. The redevelopment in turn fosters both increased transit ridership and a more vital community. Instead of the barren expanses of asphalt that surround many of the Bay Area's existing BART stations, the Colma BART Station area will become a focal point for neighborhood activity. It will facilitate transportation options by providing strategically placed pedestrian linkages, commuter drop-off areas, and new roadway connections.

The plan calls for urban housing, retail, and office uses that fit with the surrounding setting and meet demonstrated market demands. El Camino Real, currently a strip commercial street, will transition over time to a grand residential boulevard. To the west, high density housing will terrace with the form of the hills up to and around the BART station entrance. This urban housing will be designed to resemble a series of row houses or small apartment buildings, similar to those in the area now. Entries, bays, and sun porches will dot the facades, reflecting the architectural rhythm of the surrounding neighborhoods. New public parks and plazas will provide important open space amenities for residents. A pedestrian stairway, lined with retail shops, will extend from El Camino Real to the east entrance of the BART station, enticing pedestrians into a unique urban environment.

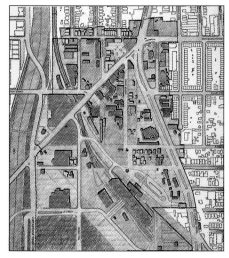

This existing conditions map shows that the site is largely built out but underutilized, with many buildings in poor condition. The area contains two schools, a major community church, the local grocery store, small shops, and various types of hous-ing. El Camino Real, the historic north-south Mission Trail of California, turns into Mission Street at this point, a symbolic shift from suburb to city.

The site is located just south of San Francisco on the new BART line to the airport. To the south of the site are the major cemeteries for the city, leading inevitably to jokes about the true nature of this transit stop.

Rio Vista West
San Diego, California

This 74 acre site is one of the first to be planned after the adoption of the TOD Design Guidelines by the City of San Diego. It is located in the fast-growing Mission Valley along the San Diego River on a new extension of the trolley. The plan integrates four primary uses into a new neighborhood: a diverse mix of housing; a variety of retail uses; a mixed-use core area at the trolley stop; and a interconnected sequence of public plazas, parks, and paths. A grid of narrow, tree-lined streets provides direct and pedestrian-friendly connections among the site's various land uses, even extending into areas typically dominated by the car.

The project incorporates three types of retail: regional, neighborhood and specialty. The specialty retail – including restaurants, cinema, major office buildings, and housing over shops – is located at the station. The regional retail component, a 120,000 sq-ft super-store complete with 700 parking stalls, is clearly out of scale with the urban qualities of the neighborhood and is typically an auto-only destination. This is a good example of the hybrid planning which must find

ways to combine the sometimes contradictory needs of transit and the pedestrian with the realities of modern auto use and retail development criteria.

Rio Vista West will contain many types of public space. A trolley plaza will serve transit users and create an active entertainment and office center. The "Crescent Commons" will provide a park with daycare, a trellised amphitheater, and rose gardens while interconnecting the housing, retail, and trolley station. The "Camino Del Este Green" will create a gateway to the site from the south while serving the residential and neighborhood commercial areas. Finally, a series of "paseos" will lead to a Riverfront Promenade that provides an active path along the river.

The plan uses a modified grid of streets, in some cases passing through the larger retail parking lots, as a way of reducing the separation of uses. Along the river are townhouses configured around courtyards, in the western corner are rental apartments, and at the center are podium apartments. Surrounding the Crescent Commons is retail with residential above and two major office buildings beyond. The trolley stop is a plaza just off the park with restaurants, cinemas, and more shops.

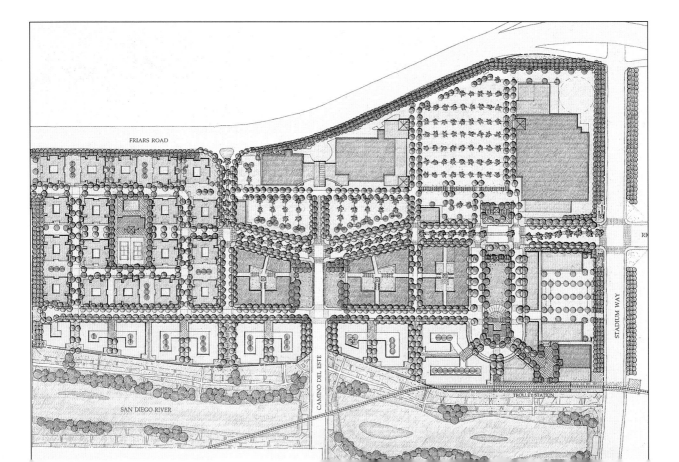

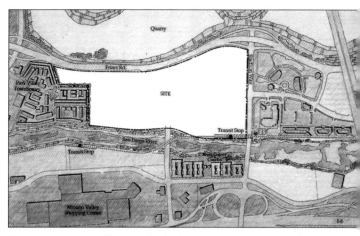

The site is close to downtown San Diego, within Mission Valley. The area is carved up by major freeways and expressways, but features a superb ecological river restoration project.

The site is surrounded by typical suburban single-use enclaves and freeways. The river and trolley line provide an opportunity for a different type of community to evolve on the site.

The plan establishes an architectural vocabulary throughout the project that emulates the work of Irving Gill. This architectural tradition is appropriate to the history and climate of the San Diego region. Strong simple forms are articulated with arcades, trellises, massive walls, shadowed windows, and tile roofs. This dignified architecture will unify the diverse elements of this new neighborhood using a vernacular style that is distinctly of San Diego.

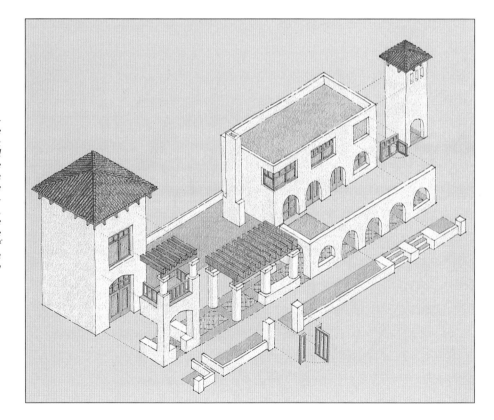

Capital River Park
Sacramento, California

Located on a 51 acre site in downtown Sacramento, Capital River Park redevelops an old cannery facility into a transit-oriented, mixed-use employment and residential center. This is another example of using a growing transit system to organize and locate jobs near the inner city. This site and its surrounding area represents, on a regional level, a prime growth area for certain segments of the housing and commercial development market. Lower density office, industrial, and housing may be appropriate farther from the city center, but high density development in this area, activated by transit, is an essential component of regional growth and diversity.

The site is configured using the old Sacramento grid and block size. Because the area is largely a deteriorating industrial district, four-story office buildings are placed at the edge to protect an inner spine of residential development. The housing is organized around a park in the north and a central pedestrian boulevard which leads to the transit plaza in the south. It is important to line the pedestrian-way with residential uses to provide 24-hour-a-day surveillance and safety. No one likes to walk through an empty neighborhood of offices late at night.

The master plan for this riverfront site proposes 1.7 million sq-ft of offices, 54,000 sq-ft of retail space, a

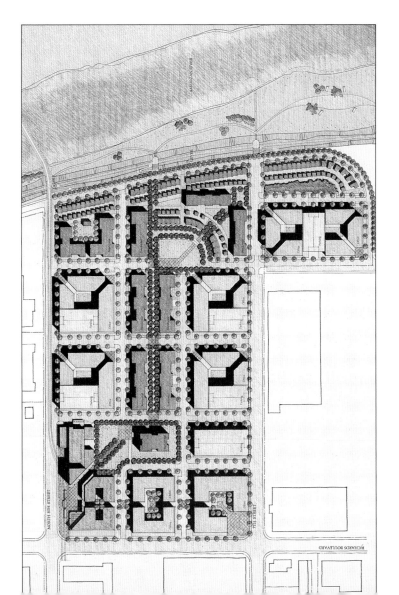

200 room hotel, and 916 townhouses and apartments in low- and mid-rise buildings. The heart of the project is an "around-the-clock" transit stop which opens onto a major pedestrian plaza lined with retail shops, restaurants, services, and the hotel. A sequence of small public plazas and parks are located along the primary pedestrian spine that links the residential component with the transit stop; tot lots, sports courts, and passive recreation areas are included as public amenities. Buildings orient to the American River Parkway with stairs, ramps, and a bikeway along the river. Capital River Park has the potential to transform an underutilized industrial area into a vibrant element of Sacramento's downtown.

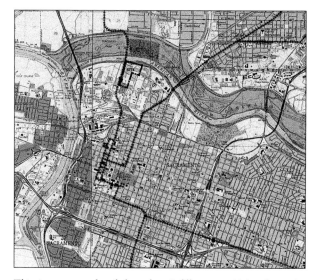

This is an example of the urban infill opportunities that exist around the older sections of our cities which were once dedicated to rail yards and complementary industrial uses. Perhaps it is appropriate that these old rail areas would give birth to a new generation of transit and its complement: walkable neighborhoods.

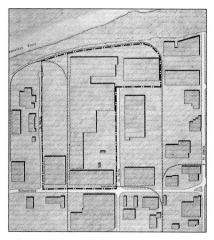

The old cannery facility, although appropriate for the historic rail and industrial district which once thrived here, is now an economic anachronism given the placement of a new light rail station.

A new city fabric with high densities can develop to match the scale of modern institutions while reflecting the urban history of the place and the needs of the pedestrian. This district is made up of buildings with a different scale and character than old Sacramento's architecture, but they represent a new generation of urban vitality and economic activity.

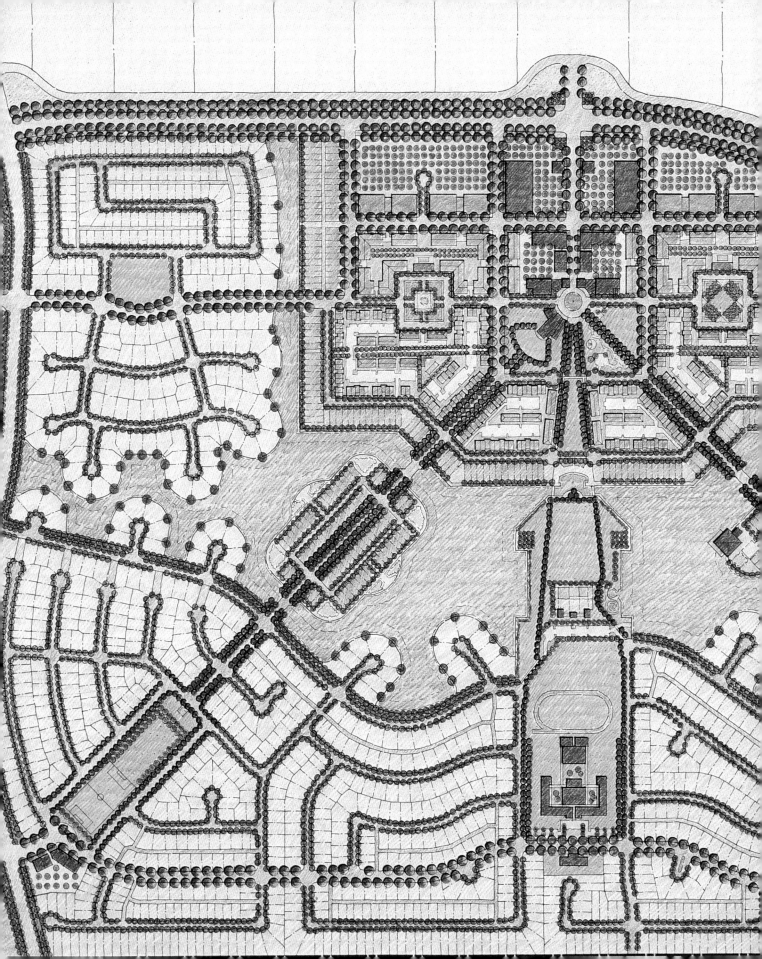

Laguna West
Sacramento, California

The design of this 800 acre site demonstrates that it is possible to reconfigure the standard elements of new growth – single-family residences, townhomes, apartments, neighborhood retail, offices, civic buildings, and recreation facilities – to enhance community, convenience, and identity. Laguna West is the first "on the ground" test of the idea the that these standard elements of growth can be modified and integrated in new ways.

The plan focuses five park-centered neighborhoods totaling 2,300 units onto a 65 acre lake, community park, and town center. The town center combines an additional 1,000 units of higher density housing with shops, offices, a village green, and urban parks. The overall community for 10,000 is designed as a traditional town in which streets are convenient and comfortable to walk, parks form a public focus, and the real life and vitality of a small town life may be rediscovered for all age groups.

The differences in the design of this community are slight and significant at the same time. The streets are narrowed, tree-lined, and connected to the town center, as well as to the arterial. At least 50 percent of the houses have front porches with garages in the rear; some are on alleyways. The mix of housing types and costs are much broader than usual, ranging from custom homes on large lots and traditional suburban single-family houses, through small-lot bungalows and townhouses, to in-law units and apartment buildings. The park system is interconnected, leading to a village green with a town hall common to all. Pedestrian promenades and bike trails boarder the lake, an amenity typically reserved for high income enclaves. The retail center is integrated with the civic uses and a transit plaza, and will feature a shop-lined Main Street.

In its first year and a half the project has completed over 200 homes, ranging in price from $120,000 to $400,000, built the lake, village green, and town hall, and attracted a major employer, Apple Computer Company. This major facility, totaling 450,000 sq-ft, represents a major shift in the suburban status quo – employers are seeking sites in mixed-use communities with transit, rather than in isolated office parks. Both jobs and housing can benefit from sharing facilities (parks, daycare, shops, and transit) which have for too long been isolated and duplicated.

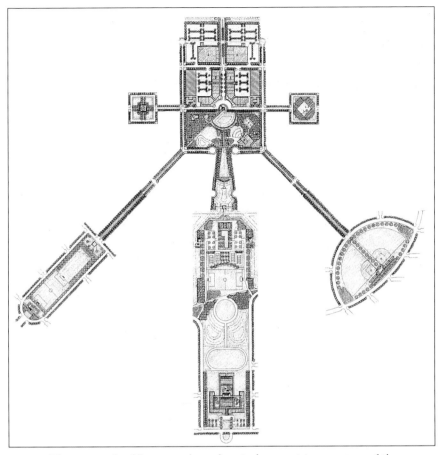

The system of public spaces shown here is the organizing structure of the community, rather than a buffer made of residual space. The town center is located at the terminus of radial boulevards which originate in neighborhood parks. A north-south civic axis is at the center of the plan, containing all the primary public uses. This radial configuration is meant to compensate for a flat, featureless site by creating a powerful focus and a grand scale.

TOWN HALL AMPHITHEATER

APPLE COMPUTER FACILITY

PORCH FRONT HOMES

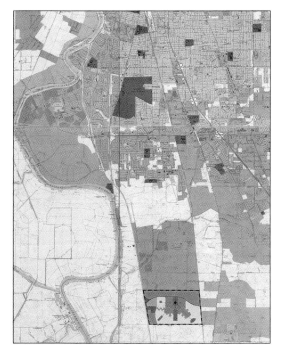

The site is located on the outer fringe of development just below the regional sewage treatment plant. Across the freeway are permanent open space, wetlands, and the Sacramento River. To the east is Laguna Creek Ranch, an area developed in standard suburban patterns just prior to Laguna West.

This street section was designed to slow traffic on the local streets and provide a more complete tree canopy. Tree-wells are located in the parking lanes of the streets.

The central civic axis contains (from bottom to top) daycare, elementary school, community recreation, pedestrian bridges, village green, town hall, transit plaza, retail, and Apple Computer, the major employer at the site. Note the configuration of the retail area: a mix of auto-oriented anchor stores on the arterial and a pedestrian-oriented Main Street off the green. It is symbolic of the attitude of the project that the most valuable property on the site is given over to community recreation and park. This area is the common ground of the diverse households included in this new neighborhood.

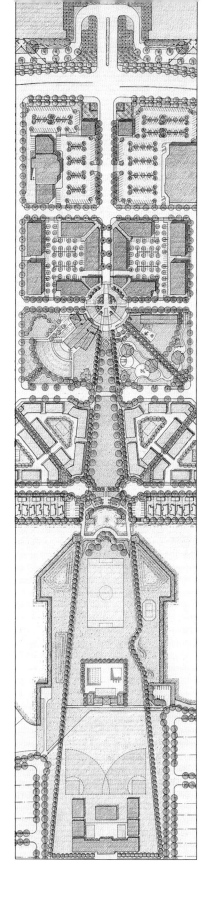

Calvine Specific Area Plan
Sacramento, California

This Specific Area Plan for the County of Sacramento establishes the framework for two mixed-use developments connected to a planned extension of the region's light rail system. The Specific Plan is an important tool in that it provides for integrated neighborhood plans across multiple property ownerships. It also provides for a common Environmental Impact Report and a financing plan for shared facilities. The Specific Plan is effectively an alternative to piecemeal, property-by-property development patterns. This is particularly relevant on a site which has 40 different ownerships ranging from two acres to 280 acres.

This plan defines a compact and integrated pattern of land use, reinforcing the use of alternative modes of transportation. The design for the northern portion of the site places major office development and an entertainment-oriented retail complex within walking distance of 1,400 homes and a light rail stop. This northern neighborhood has a mix of small-lot single-family, townhouses, and podium apartments. At its center is a triangular village green surrounded by a transit stop, daycare, and retail.

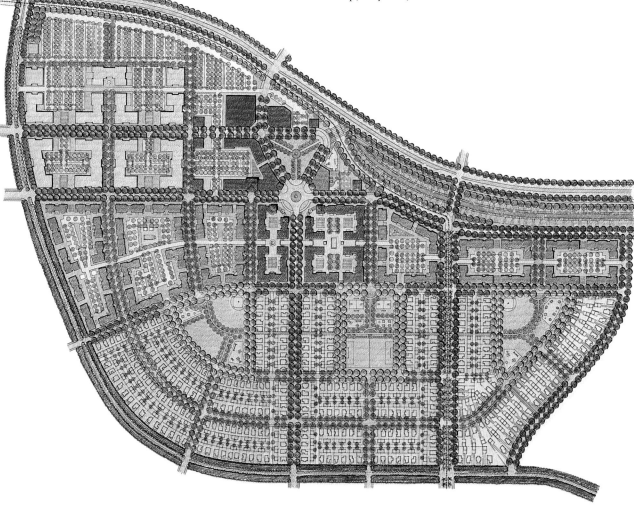

A second mixed-use area in the south of the study area is linked by feeder bus to the light rail stop and will have a community-serving retail complex within a short walk of 1,200 homes. A 20 acre community park and elementary school are located at the juncture of these two compact, pedestrian-oriented neighborhoods. The plan also establishes design guidelines and implementation measures to ensure the quality of development and to respond to specific site conditions such as wetlands, freeway noise, and special traffic needs.

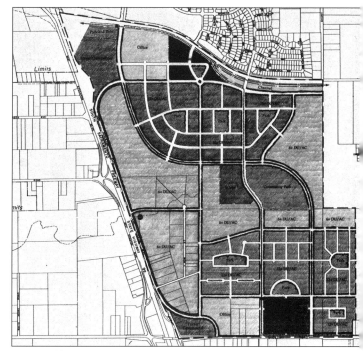

Two neighborhoods develop with a shared elementary school and major park. The area between is traditional single-family housing. The boldly lined streets are "connectors," rather than "collectors."

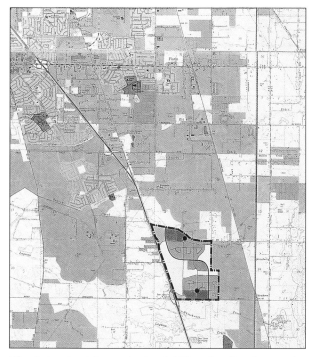

The site is a classic large suburban infill location. Development has proceeded on all surrounding sides. It has the benefit of freeway visibility and access to a new light rail station.

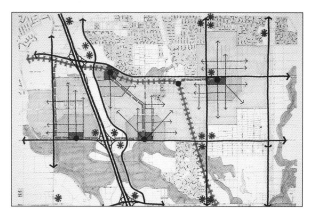

This diagram shows the placement of four new neighborhoods in relation to the light rail extension planned for this area. Each neighborhood has a street system which provides direct access to the adjacent housing while placing its retail core facing the arterial system. A feeder bus loop connects the neighborhoods to the northern light rail station. The stars represent inappropriate competing retail centers that would be rezoned.

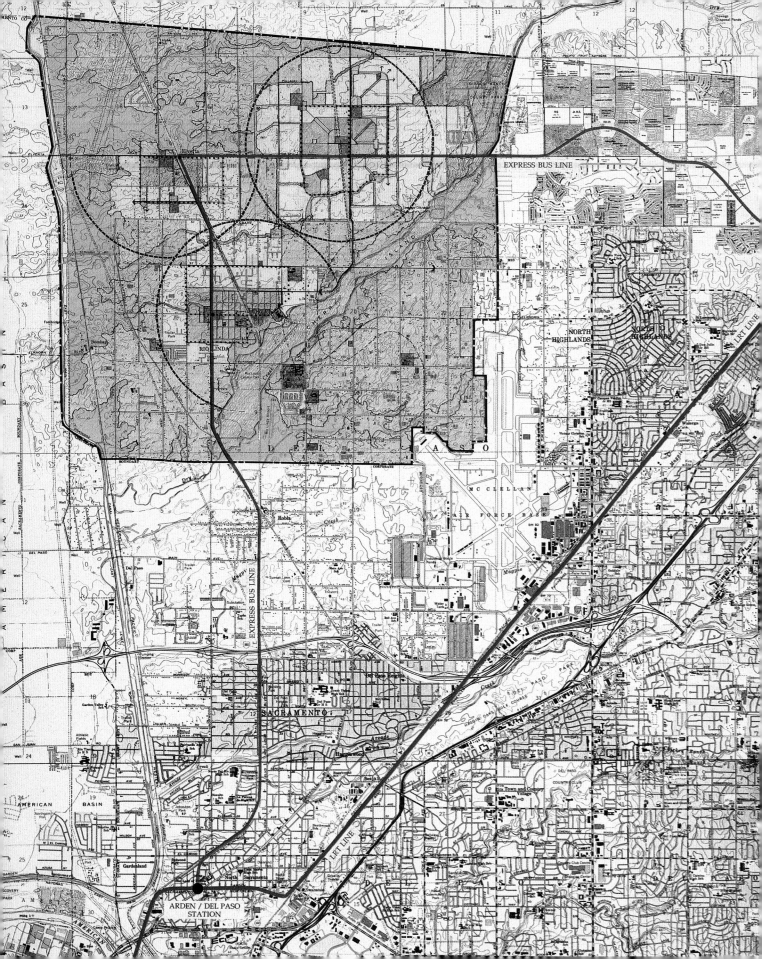

EXPRESS BUS LINE

EXPRESS BUS LINE

ARDEN / DEL PASO
STATION

Dry Creek Ranch
Sacramento, California

This plan demonstrates how a semi-rural area can grow into three distinct villages with greenbelts. The current pattern of development could easily evolve into sprawl in this relatively autonomous area north of Sacramento. Instead, three villages are proposed: one grown from a small existing town; the second a partially new, smaller hamlet near an existing postal facility; and the third a totally new village located to the east on undeveloped land, Dry Creek Ranch. Each would develop on its own timeframe, with its own character and identity.

It is a land use strategy which attempts to balance the need for the area to accept a reasonable share of regional growth, while maintaining the local community's desire to retain its rural character and lifestyle. The proposed plan maintains approximately 75 percent of

the area in open space, flood plain, and low density rural residential development to protect the existing community character. More intensively developed land uses, including retail, employment, and residential areas total 25 percent of the plan area.

The plan proposes that the existing flood plain and low intensity rural residential areas be maintained between each village as a continuous "greenbelt." A network of horse trails and bicycle paths would be located within this rural residential and open space corridor for use by the entire community. These greenbelt trails and paths would be extended into each of the villages. The new village would include a variety of housing types and provide a series of neighborhood sub-centers combining a school, park, daycare, and small country market.

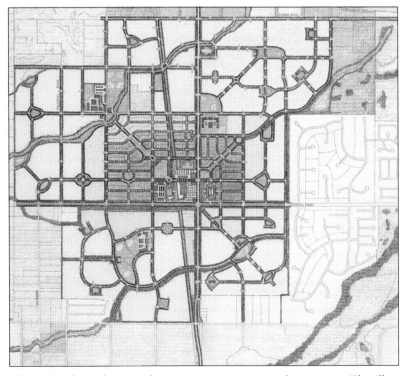

The Dry Creek Ranch master plan encompasses approximately 1,850 acres. The village is structured around a system of open space corridors and tree-lined streets emanating from the commercial core and village green. This system connects neighborhood parks, schools, and community parks with the overall community. A variety of housing types and densities will include design elements which create a small town atmosphere and maintain the rural qualities in the surrounding areas.

South Brentwood Village

Brentwood, California

At 140 acres this project represents the size of a quarter mile walking radius – and the mix and quantity of uses possible within such an area. Although smaller, denser neighborhoods are certainly possible, this plan demonstrates the diversity and breadth that a suburban site can easily incorporate in a classically walkable area. The new neighborhood focuses on a village green that is surrounded with retail shops, daycare, church, and porch-fronted homes. The project envisions a range of just over 500 new homes, including zero-lot-line carriage homes with alley-accessed garages and ancillary units. Retail stores and offices provide the local households with convenient shopping and employment opportunities.

There are several unique aspects to this neighborhood. First, it incorporates a healthy 30 percent of the site in office and commercial development. These uses line the Southern Pacific railroad tracks and the highway, creating a buffer while enhancing the site as a possible transit stop. Second, the housing is affordable and is being produced by one of the largest home builders in the State of California. This major builder is demonstrating that mixed-use, walkable neighborhoods are just as marketable as their standard subdivisions. Finally, the street system is interconnected, tree-lined and narrow – all atypical for suburban development. These streets and paths will provide the physical and visual connections between parks, homes, and shops.

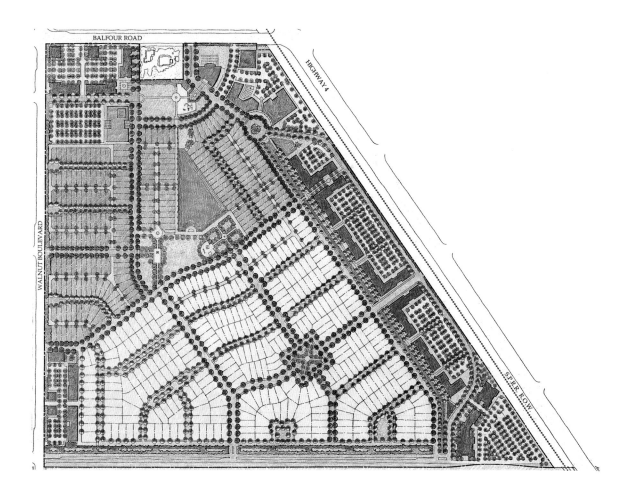

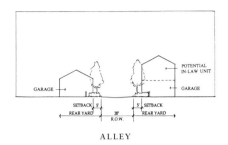

ALLEY

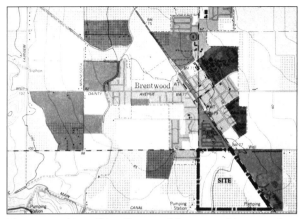

The site is within walking distance of the center of Brentwood, an old farm town with a rail stop which is now becoming a major growth area at the outer edge of the San Francisco Bay Area.

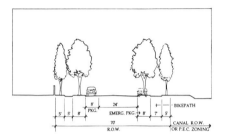

EMPLOYMENT ACCESS STREET

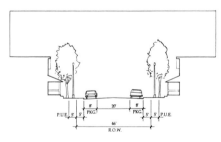

MINOR RESIDENTIAL STREET

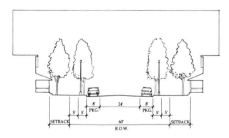

MAJOR RESIDENTIAL STREET

A variety of street sections will add diversity and identity to the neighborhood. Small mini-parks are distributed around the neighborhood for easy access.

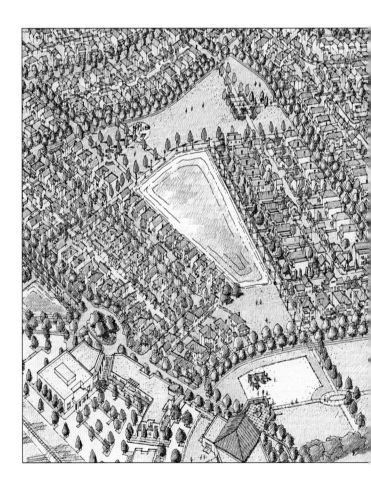

Camarillo Gateway
Camarillo, California

At approximately 250 acres and 1,200 dwelling units, the Camarillo Gateway neighborhood would be brought together around unusually extensive public and civic features, along with convenient and walkable retail areas. Open space, park land, and civic features occupy almost one-quarter of the site's total area. The central focus of the neighborhood would be a village green and community center with a theater, outdoor amphitheater, play areas, shops, cafes, daycare, and elementary school. Extending out from the green would be a 17 acre central park with a lake, boat house, playing fields, nature center, and picnic areas. In addition, an extensive trail system will pass throughout the site connecting the park, Conejo Creek, a greenbelt buffer along the freeway, and trails beyond the site. The commercial center would focus on a "Main Street" and small park, and will include a farmers market, nursery, shops, and restaurants.

The diversity of the public uses is equaled in the proposed mix of housing types. This mix will provide opportunities for a large variety of people: singles, young families, elderly, large families, owners, renters, and childless couples. Residents and visitors will walk along tree-lined streets, moving easily between homes, schools, shops, recreational facilities, civic features, transit stops, and other uses. The configuration of the neighborhood focuses on three connected public destinations: a linear park, a circular village green, and a retail center. The retail center orients to the freeway with its parking and to the community with a Main Street.

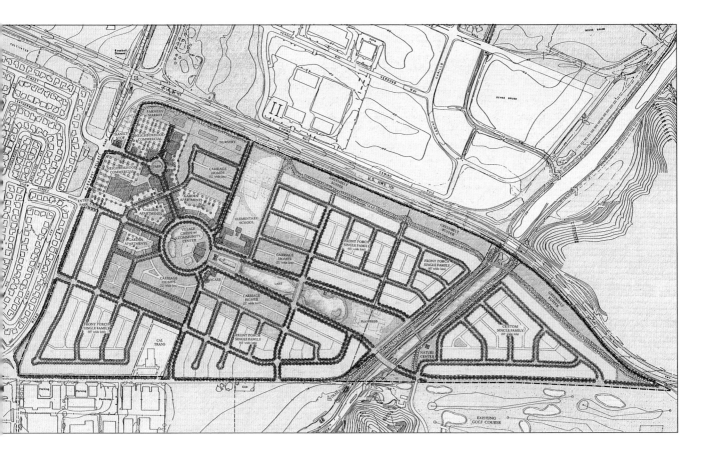

The site is controversial in that it is located at the entry to the town and is presently supporting agricultural uses. However, it is likely to be developed as it is bordered by a freeway and surrounded on 70 percent of its periphery by housing and industrial uses.

The parks and civic center of the neighborhood connect to a local creek and trail system. Its linear form puts all housing within two blocks of open space and recreation.

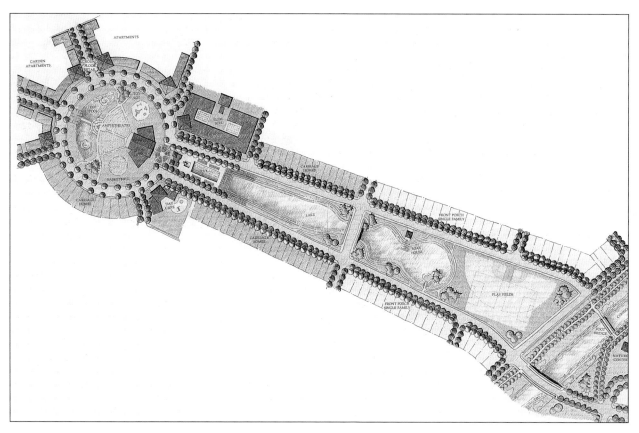

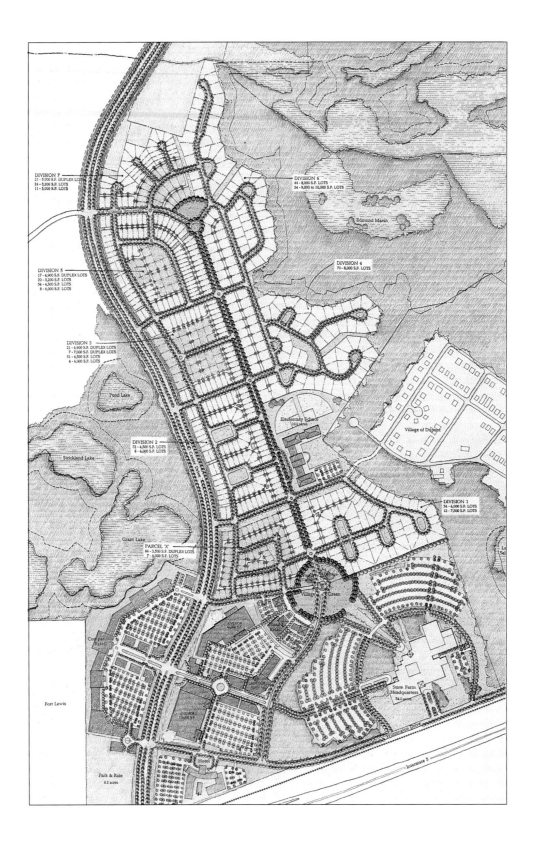

DIVISION 7
21 - 5,000 S.F. DUPLEX LOTS
24 - 3,200 S.F. LOTS
11 - 5,000 S.F. LOTS

DIVISION 6
44 - 8,000 S.F. LOTS
24 - 9,000 to 10,000 S.F. LOTS

Edmond Marsh

DIVISION 5
17 - 4,900 S.F. DUPLEX LOTS
20 - 3,200 S.F. LOTS
54 - 4,500 S.F. LOTS
8 - 6,000 S.F. LOTS

DIVISION 4
70 - 8,000 S.F. LOTS

DIVISION 3
21 - 4,900 S.F. DUPLEX LOTS
7 - 7,000 S.F. DUPLEX LOTS
31 - 4,500 S.F. LOTS
4 - 6,000 S.F. LOTS

Pond Lake

Elementary School
10 Acres

Village of Dupont

Strickland Lake

DIVISION 2
72 - 4,500 S.F. LOTS
8 - 6,000 S.F. LOTS

DIVISION 1
54 - 6,000 S.F. LOTS
12 - 7,500 S.F. LOTS

Grant Lake

PARCEL 'X'
64 - 3,500 S.F. DUPLEX LOTS
7 - 6,000 S.F. LOTS

Village Green

Comparison
Retail

ANCHOR

ANCHOR

Fort Lewis

ANCHOR
10,000 S.F.

State Farm
Headquarters
54 Acres

Hotel

Interstate 5

Park & Ride
8.2 acres

Northwest Landing

Tacoma, Washington

Northwest Landing is important because, like Laguna West, it demonstrated that mixed-use plans are attractive to major employers. State Farm Insurance Company purchased a site for a 2,000 employee facility next to the planned village green. Although they would not configure the building to directly boarder the green, they provided a strong open space connection to it – signifying the importance of sharing facilities and common ground. The Phase One plan is also a demonstration of the hybrid design which contemporary institutions require. Large-scale regional retail is configured to allow adequate parking areas, at the same time that pedestrian arcades form a continuous path from the green. Likewise, State Farm maintains visibility from the freeway while creating a connection to the town center.

The overall plan for Northwest Landing consists of three mixed-use villages located on a bluff overlooking Puget Sound and adjacent to the old company town of Dupont. The 2,100 acre site contains many archaeological and historically significant sites, including Indian settlements and one of the first trading forts in the Northwest. The overall community master plan includes 5,500 residential units, 300 acres of office development, and three "Main Street" retail areas. The configuration of the first phase is ordered around a central boulevard which allows views to the village green. The neighborhoods range from traditional single-family to alley-served cottages, each with small mini-parks.

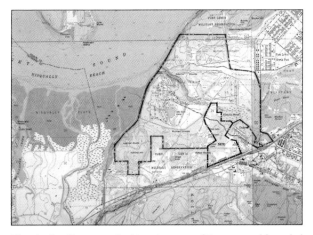

The site is adjacent to the historic town of Dupont and boarded by the Fort Lewis Military Reservation and Puget Sound, 15 miles south of Tacoma. Dupont was a company town which housed workers in their WWI and WWII explosives production.

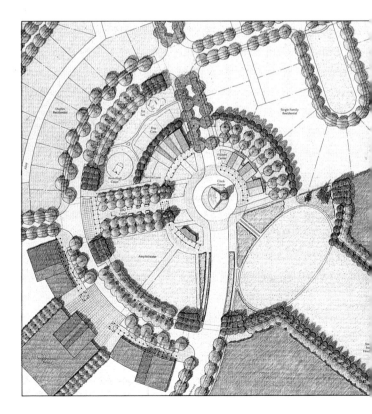

The green connects the major employer to the community's retail and housing. Within the park is a daycare center, basketball, tot lot, picnic court, and amphitheater. A grouping of shops and a visitor's center with small offices boarder the green.

Gold Country Ranch
Nevada County, California

The town's variety of housing types and densities will provide new housing opportunities affordable to a broad spectrum of families. The village green is bordered on three sides by commercial and apartments, and on the fourth side by a lake. Above the green is a community college and small-lot single-family neighborhoods. The main commercial area is flanked by office and industrial areas with a golf course. Planned for a population of 10,000, the town would also provide jobs for 8,500.

Gold Country Ranch is a proposed pedestrian-oriented "New Town" in the foothills of the Sierra just northeast of Sacramento. Unlike a satellite New Town, which is directly related by transit to a major metropolitan area, this project is designed to replicate the tradition of small, independent towns which mark this gold rush-era region. A primary purpose of the plan is to absorb growth for the area without compromising the quality of the existing towns. At the same time it seeks to preserve the quality of these towns, it emulates their rural character, historic structure, and pedestrian-scale.

This large land holding is capable of providing internal greenbelts, regional infrastructure, and affordable housing because of its low land cost. The plan for Gold Country Ranch encompasses approximately 1,750 acres of developed land, less than 25 percent of the property's 7,750 acres. The site is structured around a system of open space corridors and tree-lined streets emanating from two mixed-use town centers (only the northern town is illustrated). This system connects central town squares with neighborhood parks, schools, community parks, and the overall community. The open space corridors within the New Town will contain pedestrian, equestrian, and bicycle trails that connect to the larger preserved open spaces.

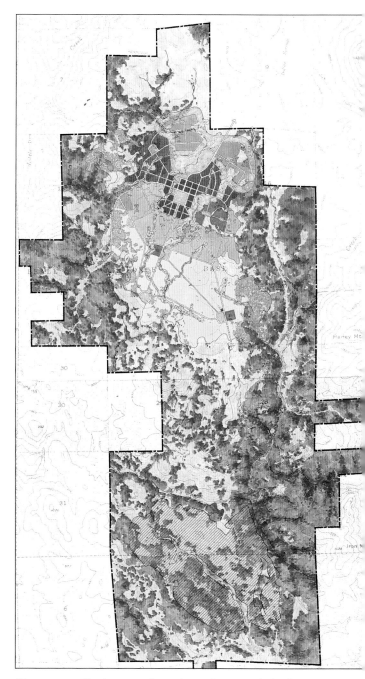

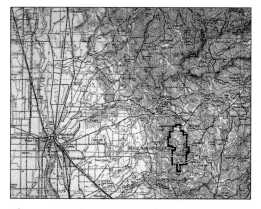

The site is in the Sierra foothills approximately 65 miles northeast of Sacramento. The existing town 10 miles east of the site is Grass Valley, an historic mining town of the gold rush era.

The conceptual land use map shows the northern town by land use areas and the southern town hatched. This is a good example of how to fit a town into complex topography. The red area is the town center with a large village green and a community college shown in blue. Two elementary schools are shown in the "Secondary Area," one adjacent to the village residential area and one farther to the south. The areas to the north of the town center are planned for various types of commercial and industrial uses.

Lexington Park
Polk County, Florida

Located on 10,000 acres in Central Florida to the east of Tampa, Lexington Park is a New Town on a proposed commuter rail line. A series of five villages and hamlets, each with a distinct character, are sited in and around significant wetlands and majestic groves of cypress. These small, relatively complete communities provide a mix of housing types, as well as recreation, entertainment, shopping, services, and employment opportunities. Some of the villages have a major retail core area with cultural and civic facilities for the entire town. Others, called hamlets, are centered on a clubhouse and convenience retail uses.

The villages will be linked to each other by a feeder bus system with connections to the commuter rail line. Even without the rail, the internal mix of housing, jobs and services resulted in a vastly reduced number of off-

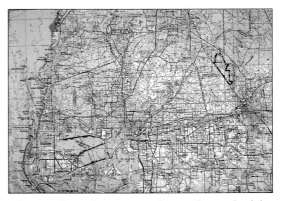

The site is located approximately 12 miles north of the town of Lakeland which is 36 miles east of Tampa. The CRX rail right-of-way boarders one side of the site and offered freight as well as commuter opportunities.

site auto trips. This plan of approximately 20,000 units of housing and 36,000 jobs demonstrates that a mixed-use New Town can create a jobs-housing balance at a scale large enough to reasonably allow a significant number of people to live and work in the same area.

The site is over 60 percent wetlands, of which only two percent were disturbed by the proposed development. Each of the villages used the wetlands both as greenbelts to define separation and as internal open space systems. The challenge was to create an efficient, interconnected street system which also avoided disturbing wetlands. In some circumstances the drainage system doubled as a series of Amsterdam-like canals lined with houses.

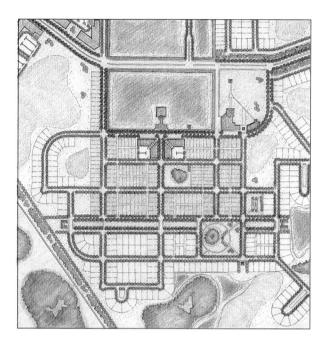

A large lake is the focus of this small hamlet, with a school to one side and a restaurant located on a pier at its center. Two small retail buildings near the pier form a gateway to the community.

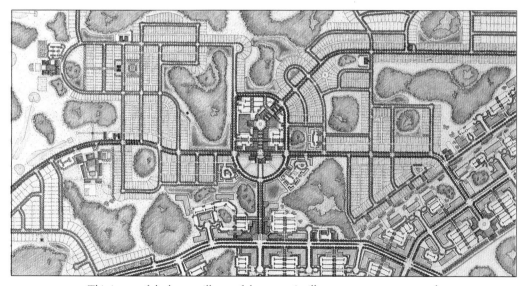

This is one of the larger villages of the town. A village green, apartments, and commercial complex is at the center, with office and light industrial buildings located one block below. The commercial center is configured with parking to the rear and a town hall at the end of the mixed-use street.

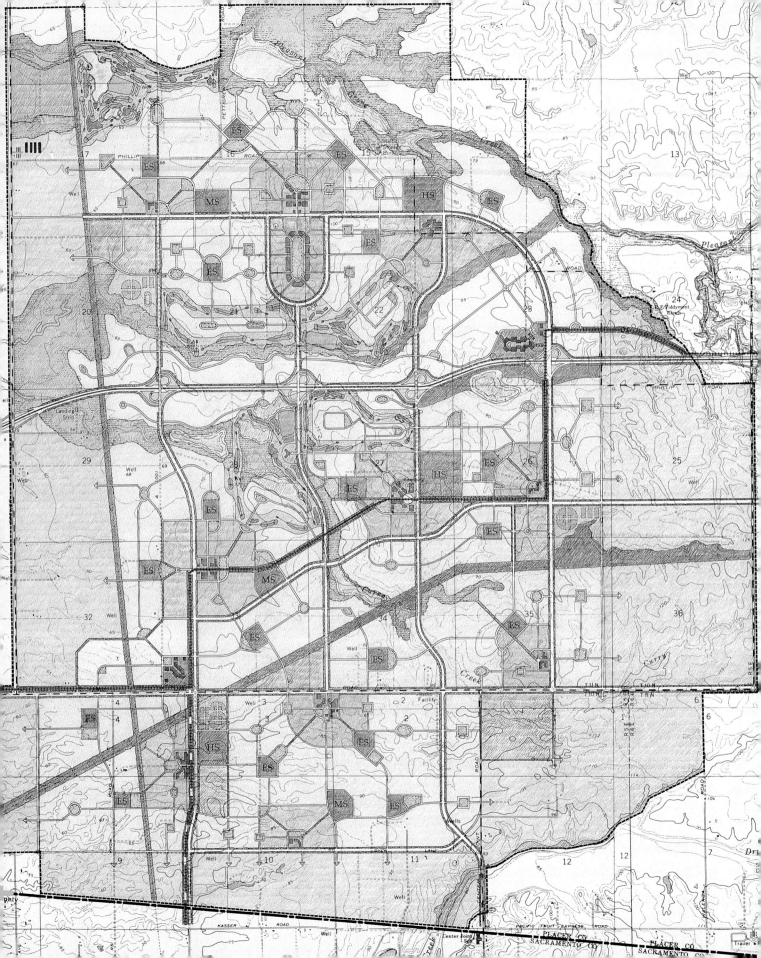

Placer Villages

Placer County, California

Placer Villages is a proposed New Town for 82,000 residents on 16,000 acres ten miles north of central Sacramento. It is a good example of an appropriate location for a satellite New Town because it is in a region with a high growth demand (700,000 over the next twenty years), it is within transit distance of the central city, it is on lands of low habitat and agricultural value, and it is well-positioned to provide part of a regional greenbelt. A project of this scale must solve many regional problems to be justified. This one will provide a light rail extension and a bypass expressway to help address regional traffic congestion problems; an ecological water and waste system to address regional water quality and supply; and a diverse and affordable mix of housing types to relieve growth pressure on overburdened existing communities.

The town contains ten villages with mixed-use cores of commercial and civic uses. A greenbelt of rural estates and aggregated community open space surrounds the town. Each village will have safe, walkable streets connecting a compact arrangement of homes, services, shopping, recreation, work, schools, and civic uses. The central northern-most village has a community college and will be developed in the latter phases of the town. A regional sewage treatment facility would provide state-of-the-art biological treatment and water reclamation for the greenbelt and open space landscaping.

Many New Towns have failed because they were not phased properly – too much infrastructure was built early in the development and the pieces did not make a whole until late in the process. The village structure of this town will allow it to grow in human-scale phases which are complete at each stage. The multiple village structure also allows different qualities in each community to emerge at the appropriate time. Earlier villages would have neighborhood-scale services and retail proportional to the pioneering population, while the latter villages, serving a larger town population, could center on a community college, regional retail, and town center civic uses.

Another important dimension of this project is its economics. New Towns such as this can afford to provide amenities, basic facilities, and services to a broad range of households because of low land costs and efficient infrastructure. In this time of municipal budget crisis and property tax limits, increasing costs are charged to new development. This, of course, either increases the cost of housing or decreases the quality of services, parks and recreation programs, schools, police, fire, or even adequate roads. Sadly, we are seeing the day in which infill, because of high land costs, developer fees, and mitigation requirements, cannot deliver affordable housing. Planning for a New Town is an alternative which can help fill the affordable housing gap.

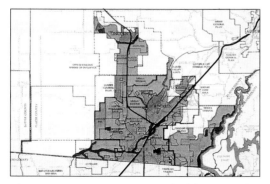

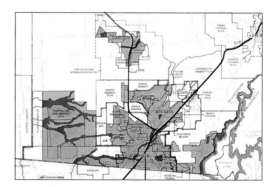

These two maps compare a "standard future" with a New Town. The total population growth for both is 120,000. The "standard future" shows the growth of what are now four distinct small towns – Roseville, Rocklin, Lincoln, and Loomis – into what could be called a freeway suburb of Sacramento. The black diagonal line is Highway 80, a primary interstate free- *way. The new growth, shown in orange, fills in between the towns with fairly expensive standard sprawl, overpowering the identity of each town. In the New Town version of the future, less growth happens around the towns, leaving open space between each and a preponderance of the "old" sections of towns. It also shifts growth away from the already congested freeway.*

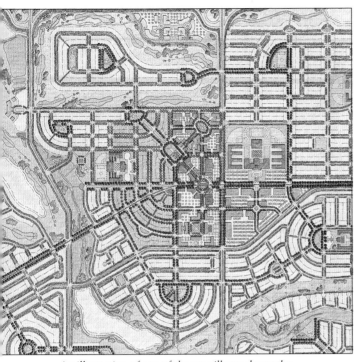

An illustration of one of the ten villages shows the detail of mixed-use and local street connections within a community. The village center has a light rail stop and retail with a radial Main Street leading to a village green. Across an arterial is an employment area and one of the town's three high schools. To the west of the village center is an elementary school which backs into a greenbelt with a stream, trails, and a golf course.

This map shows three levels of open space: regional, town-scale, and neighborhood. At the regional scale the greenbelt functions to define the edge of the metropolitan region and to permanently separate the New Town from surrounding development. The major streams provide flood protection downstream, while they allow a wildlife linkage through the urbanized area along with hiking, bike trails, and recreation. Smaller parks, often joined to schools, provide recreation, kids play areas, and community gathering points.

This pair of regional diagrams shows the location of the New Town with its road and transit connections. The site is within transit distance of the center of the metropolitan region (twelve miles is a maximum convenient travel distance at light rail speeds) and has three connections to the expanding rail system. Highway 80 is the most congested freeway in the region. The New Town location allows growth to be drawn from this overloaded corridor while it provides a relief valve to the underutilized Highway 99 on the east.

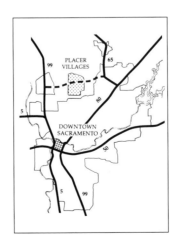

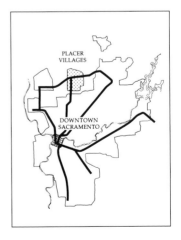

Loomis Town Center Plan
Placer County, California

This is an important example of how Transit-Oriented Development urban design principles can be applied in an existing small town – even without transit. Loomis is an old farming town which grew up around the major Southern Pacific Rail line and is now impacted by a major freeway, along with the massive growth of Sacramento, 25 miles to the southwest. The town is in danger of being consumed by the sprawling metropolis which the Sacramento region has become. Not only has Loomis attempted to avoid suburbanization with this town center plan, but it may also be protected by the construction of Placer Villages. Rather than sprawl following the freeway, Placer Villages is intended to absorb much of the growth, allowing this small town to grow at a manageable rate and in a form which honors the pedestrian.

There are several design opportunities in the town center: the infill and redevelopment of the old Main Street, the creation of a new retail center at the interchange, and the completion of the residential portions of the town center. The redevelopment of the depressed Main Street involved new landscaping treatments, identification of infill building sites, facade design guidelines, and new parking lots carved out behind the existing buildings. The new retail center had to draw people to the town and capture the tax dollars which were escaping, without competing with the old Main Street. The bridge between the two retail areas became a new civic center with library, town hall, daycare, and post office. The residential potions of the town had a variety of treatments – older neighborhoods were up-zoned to allow ancillary units and vacant parcels were zoned for townhouses and small-lot single-family. Ironically, one of the most controversial aspect of the plan was a proposal to connect two existing cul-de-sacs with the old town grid. The proposal was ultimately modified to provide a pedestrian and bike connection only.

The town has a current population of 5,700 and is surrounded by rolling Sierra foothills and old ranches. The Town of Rocklin, just to the south, doubled its size in the last ten years as a result of Sacramento's booming real estate market.

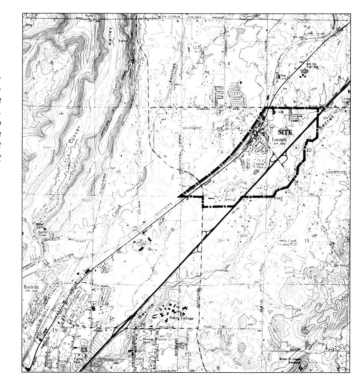

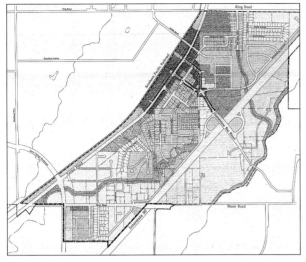

The new civic and commercial area is located just above the freeway interchange. The most controversial recommendation was to keep the area south of the freeway free of commercial development. This was intended to create a "green" entry to town.

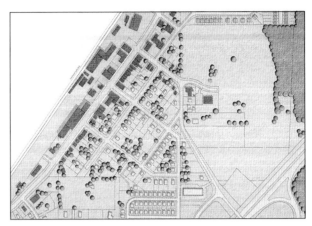

The incomplete development of the old station and Main Street area is both threatened and enticed by the development potential at the interchange.

The development of the town would balance new commercial at the freeway with infill retail on the old Main Street, new residential, and an expanded civic center and park system. The major anchor store would be visible from the freeway, but its parking area would be screened from the local streets. New housing would overlook the town park and new civic center.

Project Credits

The following is a list of Calthorpe Associates planning and urban design projects which appear in this book. Peter Calthorpe has taken the lead role in all of the projects. The other team members are listed in order of involvement.

Regional Plans

LUTRAQ: Making the Land Use, Transportation, Air Quality Connection

Portland, Oregon
1992

Client
1000 Friends of Oregon

Team
Calthorpe Associates:
Shelley Poticha (Project Manager), Philip Erickson, Catherine Chang, Joseph Scanga, Matt Taecker, and Cleve Brakefield

Cambridge Systematics
(Transportation Engineers)

Market Perspective
(Market Analysis)

Description
20 year growth plan for directing new housing and jobs into mixed-use, transit-oriented neighborhoods and revitalized downtowns in the western suburbs of Portland, Oregon.

Sacramento County Transit-Oriented Development Guidelines

Sacramento County, California
1989

Client
Sacramento County
Planning Department

Team
Calthorpe Associates:
Shelley Poticha (Project Manager), Joe Scanga, Cindy Sterry, and Catherine Chang

Mintier Associates (Implementation Recommendations)

Description
Design guidelines for directing new housing and jobs into mixed-use transit-oriented neighborhoods.

Southport Area Plan

West Sacramento, California
1991

Client
City of West Sacramento

Team
Calthorpe Associates:
Rick Williams and Philip Erickson (Project Managers), Shelley Poticha, Matt Taecker, Catherine Chang, Cleve Brakefield, Emily Keenan, and Connie Goldade

Economic and Planning Systems
(Land Economists)

Fehr & Peers Associates
(Transportation Engineers)

MacKay & Somps (Civil Engineer)

Description
7,280 acre planning area
7 Station Area Plans
2 New Neighborhoods
16,446 residential units
650,000 square feet of retail commercial
5.2 million square feet of employment (4,100 jobs)

4 community centers, 9 daycare centers, 9 hole golf course, marina facility, sensitive habitat protection in riverfront open space corridor, 9 elementary schools, 2 middle schools, high school, light rail, and feeder bus system.

San Diego
Design Guideline

San Diego, California
1991

Client
City of San Diego

Team
Calthorpe Associates:
Shelley Poticha (Project Manager),
Matt Taecker, Catherine Chang,
and Joseph Scanga

Description
Design guidelines for directing new
housing and jobs into mixed-use
transit-oriented neighborhoods. Illustrative Plans for three neighborhoods.

Merced Villages

Merced, California
1991

Client
The City of Merced

Team
Calthorpe Associates:
Matt Taecker and Shelley Poticha
(Project Managers), Catherine Chang

Economic and Planning Systems
(Land Economists)

Fehr & Peers Associates
(Transportation Engineers)

Description
7,900 acre Regional Plan

9 villages
25,000 residential units
890,000 square feet of retail
    commercial
1.3 million square feet of employment
    (5,200 jobs)

Daycare centers, 10 elementary
schools, 3 middle schools, 3 high
schools, community college expansion,
potential University of California
Campus, village, neighborhood, and
community parks, trail system, light
rail, and bus system.

Station Area Plans

Atlantic Center

Brooklyn, New York
1986

Client
Rose Associates

Team
Calthorpe Associates: Eric Carlson

Skidmore, Owing & Merrill
(Architecture and Planning)

Description
24 acre mixed-use Station Area Plan
641 residential units
800,000 square feet of retail
    commercial
2.7 million square feet of employment
    (7,700 jobs)

Daycare center, community center, and
subway station.

Jackson-Taylor
Revitalization Strategy

San Jose, California
1991

Client
City of San Jose

Team
Calthorpe Associates:
Shelley Poticha (Project Manager),
Rick Williams, and Cindy Sterry

Bay Area Economics (Economists)

Description
75 acre Station Area Plan
2,155 residential units
106,625 square feet of retail
    commercial
633,000 square feet of employment
    (2,500 jobs)

Daycare center, community center,
cultural center, expanded neighborhood park, small parks and plazas,
and BART station.

Colma BART
Specific Area Plan

Daly City and San Mateo County,
California
1991

Client
San Mateo County, Daly City,
and SamTrans

Team
Calthorpe Associates:
Shelley Poticha (Project Manager),
Rick Williams, Matt Taecker,
Joseph Scanga, and David Arkin

David E. Miller
(Project Management and EIR)

Bay Area Economics (Economists)

Fehr & Peers Associates
(Transportation Engineers)

Zigterman Engineering
(Civil Engineer)

Description
110 acre Station Area Plan
1,075 residential units
269,700 square feet of retail
    commercial
353,300 square feet of employment
    (1,384 jobs)

Daycare center, church, fire station,
2 elementary schools, neighborhood
park, public plazas, pedestrian stairway,
BART station, park-n-ride facility, bus
transfer stop, and 3 kiss-n-ride facilities.

Rio Vista West

San Diego, California
1992

Client
CalMat Properties Company

Team
Calthorpe Associates:
Matt Taecker (Project Manager)
and Joseph Scanga

Turrini & Brink
(Implementation and Planning)

Bement, Dainwood & Sturgeon
(Civil Engineer)

Entranco-Federhart
(Transportation Engineers)

Douglas Newcomb, Inc.
(Landscape Architect)

Description
95 acre Station Area Plan
1,070 residential units
325,000 square feet of retail
    commercial
165,000 square feet of employment
    (660 jobs)

Daycare center, community center,
cinema, riverfront promenade, village
commons, and light rail station.

Capital River Park

Sacramento, California
1990

Client
Goodell & Associates and
Lodi Mission Partners

Team
Calthorpe Associates:
Rick Williams (Project Manager),
Philip Erickson, and Joseph Scanga

Description
52 acre Station Area Plan
916 residential units
54,000 square feet of retail commercial
1.7 million square feet of employment
    (6,800 jobs)

600 room hotel, riverfront promenade
and light rail stop.

New Neighborhoods

Laguna West

Sacramento County, California
River West Developments

Designed
1989

Team
Calthorpe Associates: Joe Scanga,
Mark Macy, Jan Lee Wong, and
Philip Erickson

Ken Kay Associates
(Landscape Architecture)

Fehr & Peers Associates
(Transportation Engineers)

Jack Mixon (Land Planning)

The Spink Corporation
(Civil Engineers)

Description
1,033 acre mixed-use New
    Neighborhood
3,353 residential units
180,000 square feet of retail
    commercial
2.7 million square feet of employment
    (5,000 jobs)

Town hall, daycare center, elementary
school, neighborhood parks, village
green, express bus stop, and feeder bus
network.

Laguna West Town Hall

Sacramento County, California
1989

Client
River West Developments

Team
Calthorpe Associates: Joseph Scanga,
Paul Okomoto, Cleve Brakefield,
Rick Williams, Cindy Sterry, and
Christina Freidrich

KenKay Associates
(Landscape Architecture)

Rogers-Ludke (Structural Engineers)

Peters Engineers (Mechanical/
Plumbing/Electrical Engineers)

The Spink Corporation (Civil)

Carla Carstens Design (Interiors)

Description
12,000 square foot multi-purpose
    building

Classrooms, library, kitchen, multi-
purpose room, indoor/outdoor stage,
and adjacent amphitheater.

Calvine Specific Area Plan

Sacramento County, California
1990

Client
Sacramento County Planning
Department

Team
Calthorpe Associates:
Shelley Poticha and Matt Taecker
(Project Managers), Cindy Sterry

Deakin, Harvey, Skabardonis
(Transportation Planning)

MacKay & Somps (Civil Engineer)

Mogavero & Associates
(Public Involvement)

Description
615 acre project area
1 Station Area Plan
1 New Neighborhood
　Secondary Area
3,470 residential units
540,000 square feet of retail
　commercial
790,000 square feet of employment
　(3,200 jobs)

Daycare center, elementary school,
20 acre community park, light rail
stop, and feeder bus network.

Dry Creek Ranch

Sacramento County, California
1991

Client
Dry Creek Ranch Ownership Group

Team
Calthorpe Associates:
Rick Williams (Project Manager),
Philip Erickson, Catherine Chang,
Joseph Scanga, and Christina Freidrich

Economic and Planning Systems
(Land Economists)

Fehr & Peers Associates
(Transportation Engineers)

MacKay & Somps (Civil Engineer)

Description
2,260 acre project area
2 Infill Neighborhoods
1 New Neighborhood
8,000 residential units
160,000 square feet of retail
　commercial
300,000 square feet of employment
　(1,200 jobs)

Town hall, daycare center, equestrian
trails, 3 elementary schools, and
express bus and feeder bus networks.

South Brentwood Village

Brentwood, California
1991

Client
South Brentwood Associates/
Kaufman & Broad

Team
Calthorpe Associates:
Rick Williams (Project Manager),
Philip Erickson, Joseph Scanga,
Matt Taecker, Catherine Chang,
Christina Freidrich, and Paul Okomoto

Carlson, Barbee & Gibson
(Civil Engineer)

Description
140 acre New Neighborhood
522 residential units
114,300 square feet of retail
commercial
215,600 square feet of employment
(860 jobs)

Daycare center, church, and
neighborhood park.

Camarillo Gateway

Camarillo, California
1992

Client
The Sammis Company

Team
Calthorpe Associates:
Matt Taecker (Project Manager),
Joseph Scanga, Catherine Chang,
and Rick Williams

South Bay Engineering (Civil Engineer)

Market Perspectives (Market Analysis)

Moore Iacofano Goltsman
(Public Meeting Facilitation)

Description
250 acre New Neighborhood
1,200 residential units
180,000 square feet of retail
　commercial

Community center, daycare center,
pool, nature center, farmer's market,
community gardens, elementary
school, and feeder bus station.

Northwest Landing

Dupont, Pierce County, Washington
1990

Client
Weyerhauser Real Estate Company

Team
Calthorpe Associates:
Philip Erickson (Project Manager),
Rick Williams, Joe Scanga,
Christina Freidrich, Catherine Chang,
and David Arkin

ESM, Inc. (Civil Engineers)

Robert Shinbo Associates
(Landscape Architects)

Mithune Partners
(Architectural Consultants)

Description
2,100 acre New Town
3 villages
5,500 residential units
1.8 million square feet of retail
　commercial
9 million square feet of employment
　(36,000 jobs)

Town hall, daycare center,
6 elementary schools, 3 middle
schools, and 2 high schools.

Towns and New Towns

Gold Country Ranch

Nevada County, California
1991

Client
Gold Country Ranch Inc.

Team
Calthorpe Associates:
Philip Erickson (Project Manager),
Catherine Chang, Matt Taecker,
and Maya Foty

Eugene Dvorak (Client Representative)

Economic and Planning Systems
(Land Economists)

Omni Means and MacKay &d Somps
(Civil Engineers)

Fehr & Peers Associates
(Transportation Engineers)

Description
7,750 acre New Town
2 villages
7,385 residential units
615,200 square feet of retail
    commercial
1.4 million square feet of employment
    (550 jobs)

Town hall, daycare center, college,
18 hole golf course, 3 elementary
schools, 2 middle schools, 100 acres of
town squares, neighborhood parks,
and community parks, 6,000 acres of
preserved open space.

Lexington Park

Polk County, Florida
1989

Client
Flag Development Company

Team
Calthorpe Associates:
Rick Williams (Project Manager),
Joe Scanga, and Philip Erickson

Dames & Moore
(Transportation Engineering)

Envisors, Inc. (Civil Engineering)

Conservation Consultants, Inc.
(Environmental)

Fishkind & Associates, Inc.
(Market Economics)

Description
10,000 acre New Town
7 villages
20,000 residential units
1.8 million square feet of retail
    commercial
9 million square feet of employment
    (36,000 jobs)
Town hall, daycare center,
6 elementary schools, 3 middle schools,
and 2 high schools, commuter rail stop,
and feeder bus network.

Placer Villages

Placer County, California
1991

Client
Placer Village Associates

Team
Calthorpe Associates
Philip Erickson (Project Manager),
Cindy Sterry, Catherine Chang, and
Matt Taecker

Economic and Planning Systems
(Land Economists)

Fehr & Peers Associates
(Transportation Engineers)

MacKay & Somps (Civil Engineer)

AgAccess (Soils)

PACE (Ecological Systems)

Description
16,040 acre New Town
10 villages
34,175 residential units
3 million square feet of retail
    commercial
19 million square feet of employment
    (32,000 jobs)

Town hall, daycare center,
19 elementary schools, 3 middle
schools, 3 high schools,community
college, 18 hole golf course,
neighborhood and community parks,
light rail system, and feeder bus
network.

Loomis Town Center Plan

Loomis, California
1991

Client
Town of Loomis

Team
Calthorpe Associates:
Matt Taecker and Shelley Poticha
(Project Managers), Cindy Sterry,
and Catherine Chang

Mintier Associates
(Implementation Recommendations)

Deakin, Harvey & Skabardonis
(Transportation Planners)

Moore Iacofano Goltsman
(Public Meeting Facilitation)

Description
490 acre Town Center Plan
750 new residential units
250,000 new square feet of retail
    commercial
220,000 new square feet of
    employment (1,500 jobs)

Town hall, central park, community
center, daycare center, existing
elementary school.

Illustration Credits

Cover

Bird's Eye Perspective,
Rick Williams, 1990

The Next American Metropolis

P. 18
Household Composition,
US Census, 1990

P. 19
Distribution of Bay Area Office Space,
Gary Pivo

P.27
Transit Stop Illustration, Mark Mack,
"The Pedestrian Pocket Book,"
Kelbaugh, et al, Princeton
Architectural Press, 1989

P.32
Portland Regional Light Rail System,
City of Portland Office of
Transportation, Portland, Oregon

P. 33
Contemporary City, Le Corbusier,
"Urban Utopias in the Twentieth
Century," Robert Fishman, MIT Press,
Cambridge Massachusetts, 1982

P.33
Welwyn Garden City, E. Howard and
L. de Soissons, "Genesis of Welwyn
Garden City: Some Jubilee Memories,"
Frederic J. Osborn, Broadwater Press,
Welwyn Garden City

P.33
Broadacre City, F. L. Wright, "Urban
Utopias in the Twentieth Century,"
Robert Fishman, MIT Press,
Cambridge Massachusetts, 1982

P. 35
Annual VMT, "Explaining Urban
Density and Transit Impacts on
Auto Use," John Holtzclaw,
Natural Resources Defense Council
and Sierra Club, 1991

Guidelines

P. 44
Radburn, C.S. Stein,
"Towards New Towns for America,"
MIT Press, Cambridge, 1973

P. 45
The Pedestrian Pocket,
"The Pedestrian Pocket Book,"
Kelbaugh, et al, Princeton
Architectural Press, 1989

P. 47
Growth Trends: 1969 – 1990, US
Census, 1990

P. 47
Modal-Split, John Pucher,
"Urban Travel Behavior as the
Outcome of Public Policy,"
AICP Journal, Autumn 1988

P. 48
Daily Trip Generation in
the San Francisco Bay Area,
Fehr & Peers Associates, 1992

P. 49
Conventional Suburban vs. Traditional
Neighborhood Development,
Walter Kulash, et al "Traditional
Neighborhood Development: Will the
Traffic Work?," Prepared for the
American Society of Civil Engineers,
1990

P. 83
Housing Types Diagrams,
Sam Davis, "The Form of Housing,"
Van Nostrand Reinhold Company,
New York, 1977

P. 90
Parks, Plaza, and Civic Buildings,
Mark Mack, "The Pedestrian Pocket
Book," Kelbaugh, et al, Princeton
Architectural Press, 1989

P. 109
Joint Use Parking, Urban Land
Institute, "Shared Parking,"
Washington D.C., 1983